The 12 Gifts of Life

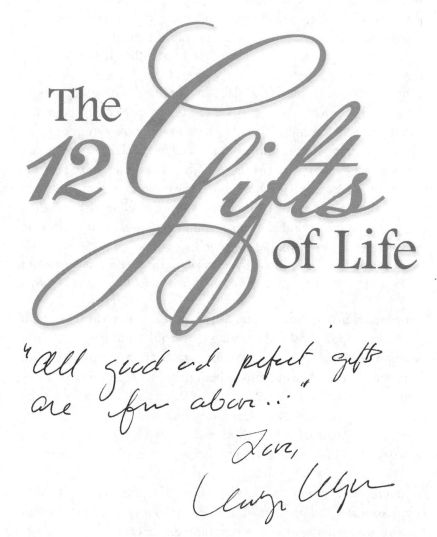

"All good and perfect gifts
are "from above..."

Love,

[signature]

Advance Praise for *The Twelve Gifts of Life…*

"Cindy Champnella seizes 'ordinary' moments and recalibrates them with God's yardstick. The result? An immeasurably poignant read that spans seas and family secrets and will soften the heart of even the most persnickety person in your sphere of influence!"
—Patti Lacy, author of *Reclaiming Lily*

"I think each of us has hit a place in our lives when we wonder if what we are doing and who we are really matter. This amazing book by Cindy Champnella lets us share in her exploration of those questions and join in the journey for ourselves. Each of us has a mark to make and gifts to give. *The Twelve Gifts of Life* allows us to see how abundant our lives are and how much meaning they have, not only for ourselves, but for every other life we touch. Cindy has touched many lives, mine included. After reading this book, you will come away changed, and thank her for touching yours."
—Carrie Kitze, Publisher EMK Press and author of *We See the Moon* and *I Don't Have Your Eyes*

"For generations to come, readers will be quoting from *The Twelve Gifts of Life*, the inspirational and uplifting new book from favorite, Cindy Champnella. This is a vital and unforgettable reading experience for everyone….Cindy has the gift of being able to see ordinary family events as extraordinary, events to be treasured and held close for the treasures they are. Cindy's talent for giving these events a new life, enables us to change how we think and opens a whole new world of understanding and thanksgiving for being a part of the experience.

A superb and deeply emotional book, Champnella is at once compassionate and incisive. *The Twelve Gifts of Life*, through its honesty and conviction, is a rich reading experience."
—Richard Fischer, Publisher of Adoption Today and Fostering Families Today magazines

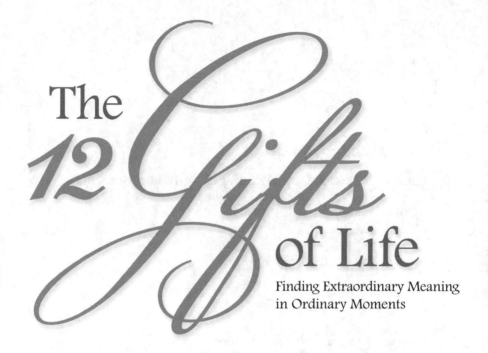

The 12 Gifts of Life

of Life

Finding Extraordinary Meaning
in Ordinary Moments

Cindy Champnella, PhD

AMBASSADOR INTERNATIONAL
GREENVILLE, SOUTH CAROLINA & BELFAST, NORTHERN IRELAND

www.ambassador-international.com

The Twelve Gifts of Life

Finding Extraordinary Meaning in Ordinary Moments

Printed in the United States of America

ISBN: 978-1-62020-048-3
eISBN: 978-1-62020-049-0

Cover Design by Rita Golden of Confluence Graphics
Page Layout by Kelley Moore of Points & Picas

AMBASSADOR INTERNATIONAL
Emerald House
427 Wade Hampton Blvd.
Greenville, SC 29609, USA
www.ambassador-international.com

AMBASSADOR BOOKS
The Mount
2 Woodstock Link
Belfast, BT6 8DD, Northern Ireland, UK
www.ambassador-international.com

The colophon is a trademark of Ambassador

Dedication

To Jaclyn
For your amazing courage in
allowing me to tell your story.
Don't think for a minute that I don't
realize what that has cost you.
Because of you, so many lives have
been forever changed,
Including my own.

and

To Joe
For your amazing courage in choosing to love us.
Don't think for a minute that I don't
realize what that has cost you.
Because of you, I finally found what
I had searched a lifetime for.
In you, I found me.

More Advance Praise for *The Twelve Gifts of Life*...

"I loved this book. Reading it was like getting hit over the head with a tidal wave of thought, observation, wisdom and emotion. Cindy Champnella is just like me, only better! I easily relate to her story and the challenges she has faced (international adoption, parenting a child with trauma, divorce, working single parenthood), but her story flies on wings of faith and hope and her challenges work to strengthen her resolve. I am not left behind, however, because *The 12 Gifts of Life, Finding Extraordinary Meaning in Ordinary Moments* lets us all experience the insight, clarity and miracles that have shaped Cindy's aptitude for appreciation, and helps us clearly understand that we all hold our own perceptive key to truly conscious living.

Dr. Champnella's family is integral to her discovery of the 12 gifts, and her children sharply outline some of Cindy's most important life lessons with humor, spirit and brutal honesty. Motherhood is life-altering; for Cindy (and for those of us touched by her writing) motherhood is also world-changing. The author's 13th gift to her readers is the fact that she generously shares her close-to-the-heart, "ordinary moment" life lessons with each of us, and that seeing ourselves in Cindy, we recognize how to gain, use and value the extraordinary 'ordinary' in our own worlds, too."
—Jean MacLeod, author of *At Home in This World* and author & co-editor of *Adoption Parenting: Creating a Toolbox, Building Connections*

"Cindy's first book, *The Waiting Child* riveted audiences with its powerful story of love and hope as told through her daughter Jaclyn's desperate journey for reunification with her beloved orphanage charge. Now, Champnella is sharing how motherhood, the adoption of her children and her life journey has forever changed her and shares the gifts of wisdom she has received on her life journey. These are stories of everyday miracles and the power of love, forgiveness and commitment. *The 12 Gifts of Life* is a great read and will leave a profound impact on the reader."
—Kim Hansel, Editor of Adoption Today and Fostering Families Today magazines; Editor of *The Foster Parenting Toolbox*.

Contents

Preface

When I was in my early twenties, I heard middle-aged women talk wistfully about how they wished they had known back then— when they were my age—what they knew now. The implication was that wisdom only comes with age and that knowledge extracts a heavy price in exchange: your youth. I couldn't stand those women. I thought it sad—and puzzling too—that they had been so naïve when they were young.

I considered myself pretty savvy. I was educated, after all. Always at the top of my class. And I was riding the cusp of the women's movement. I felt sorry that these older women had missed out.

It never occurred to me to ask them for advice. And had they offered any, I would have smiled indulgently and then ignored it. After all, their experiences were different from mine. It was a different time, a new generation. My generation was filled with possibilities that these women didn't have in their day.

What I didn't understand then was that although lifestyles change, technology constantly propels us forward, knowledge explodes, and our world grows ever more complex, people stay the same. We try. We fail. We try again. We learn from our mistakes—hopefully. We love. We get hurt. We love again. We hope. We are disappointed. We still believe.

As it is with most of us, my life is the intersection of many different roles—I am a wife, a mother, a daughter, a college administrator, a psychologist, a volunteer, and a woman of faith. The dizzying combination of these different roles has given me more questions than answers. I have had a lifetime of experiences, and these have shaped me too. I am divorced and re-married. I gave birth to Kate and later adopted both Christy and Jaclyn from China. I finished graduate school when I was fifty. I have walked away from jobs that challenged my integrity and stayed too long in ones that bored me to death. I am now one of those middle-aged women. I have that wisdom that only comes with age—the knowledge that takes root and grows in the fertile soil of our failures. I've learned that life grabs hold of you, like a rip-tide after a storm, and pulls you under. If you don't drown in sorrow, debt, heartache, or bitterness—and many do—you will emerge from the current. You'll find yourself on the other side of fifty, not only more resilient but also wiser. With lots of cellulite! And plenty of regrets.

Sometimes I wish I could do something noble and wonderful with all this hard-earned wisdom I've gleaned. Then I remember that young woman from years ago, and I know that any attempt I make to share my wisdom will be met with the same disdain I had for those who preceded me.

I once asked my middle-aged friends, "If you could go back in time and talk to your twenty-year-old selves, what would you say?"

"I'd tell her to have more than one child," said Pat, a highly successful senior executive. "And to buy Microsoft stock. That would pretty much take care of the rest."

"I'd tell her to take chances," said stay-at-home mom Sasha. "And to travel. I'd also encourage her to say no to people more often. I'd tell her that no doesn't make people hate you; it makes them respect you more. That's true even with your kids."

"I'd tell her not to be so hard on herself when she's doing the best she can," added Cheri, a fellow over-worked and under-appreciated school administrator still reeling from the recent loss of her beloved father. "And I'd tell her always to end conversations with 'I love you.' While you still have the time."

You break the sacred rules of girlfriend equity if you ask a question you aren't willing to answer yourself. But I struggled with this one, maybe because my list of regrets was so long.

After some contemplation, I decided I'd give my younger self these pieces of advice.

• Marry someone kind.

Over the long haul, kind trumps good-looking every time. Kind trumps smart too. And successful. And charming. Kind trumps everything. Kind goes the distance.

• Understand fear.

Most people are afraid. What each person fears is different—for some it's failure, for others it's a lifetime battle with a sense of unworthiness. For some it's a fear of being alone.

The most obnoxious braggarts and the biggest jerks are the ones who are most afraid. Understanding that fact is the key to dealing with the bullies in life and also to tamping down your own fear.

- The only way to receive anything of true value in life is to give.

This is the most amazing truth in life—but it's so counterintuitive that many people never get it.

I really understood this one after I adopted my first child from China. In the beginning I had been motivated by a desire to give back. I had a life full of blessings. By adopting one family-less child, I thought I could, in some small way, tilt the seesaw of inequity in life.

The ridiculousness of this became apparent when well-meaning strangers applauded my virtuousness by saying things like, "What a lucky baby! You did such a wonderful thing to adopt her." What? Lucky baby? She was beautiful and smart and charming and loveable and the joy of my life. I was the lucky one. Then it clicked. When you give love, you get back a million times what you give. The reverse is also true. If you are stingy with love, your own heart will echo with emptiness.

This concept works with just about everything in life. The only way to have real joy is to spread joy. The only way to have positive relationships with people, to authentically connect at an emotional level, is to put yourself out there. To risk rejection. To risk heartache. To risk betrayal. But you'll gain everything.

- Don't be impatient with others.

Everyone has gifts and talents, and we can no more take credit for them than we can take credit for the color of our eyes. As a result, there is a person for every job. Work that would bore one person to death fascinates another. No gift is superior to another.

And remember, most people are doing the best they can, so stop sighing deeply when others don't do things to your satisfaction.

- Who we are has nothing to do with our work or our job title.

I'd tell my younger self not to let others categorize her. Only you can truly value yourself. So treat yourself as valuable.

- The tough things in life—the experiences we try to avoid—have a deeper purpose.

Character is built and revealed in our adversity, not in our triumphs. When you've lost your job and use your unexpected free time to volunteer, when you invite someone you don't really like that much to join your group for lunch, when you leave a generous tip, when you return extra change, when you don't have to have the last word even when you're right—these are the moments that matter. Character is the sum of our smallest actions.

- Where you spend your money and your time reflects your investment in life.

If you invest in a nice house, you will be rewarded with beautiful surroundings. If you invest in shopping, you will be rewarded with a beautiful outward appearance (and a bulging closet). But if you invest in children, you will have a beautiful life. If you invest in service to others, you will have a beautiful heart. If you invest in believing, you will have a beautiful soul.

This one is hard to understand when you're staring into the seemingly endless vistas of your twenties, so I'd warn my younger self that there is only so much time. When tomorrow comes, our regrets will be about things we wished we'd done, the opportunities we passed up, the things we thought we'd have time to do later in life but never did. If you wait for the perfect time to do something, if you wait for enough money to do it comfortably, you'll likely miss out. Jump.

• Value kindness.

I'd end back where I began. I'd make sure my younger self understood that the greatest compliment in life is not "You are successful" or "You are famous" or "You are rich." None of those goals are ultimately satisfying. The greatest compliment someone can give you is "You are kind." If you focus on this goal, the rest will pretty much fall into place. In the end, kind wins.

Would I trade all this hard-earned wisdom for the cellulite-free thighs I had in my twenties? Maybe. Would I want to go through all the experiences needed to figure it all out again? Unthinkable.

The truth is that most of us never get a chance to make our mark of greatness on the world—which doesn't negate our basic human desire to find meaning in our stories. Maybe what we fear most in life isn't some terrible tragedy befalling us but that our life will be ordinary. And then there are the questions: How do we hold onto hope when all indicators point to floundering financial futures? How do we feel joy in a society of failing families and Facebook-limited friendships? How do we find purpose when paying the bills has to be our priority? How do we believe when God is silent? How do we know that our lives *really* matter? If you've ever asked any of these questions, it is my hope that *The Twelve Gifts of Life* will alter your perspective.

Each of our lives is really a collection of stories—the totality of which has shaped who we are. This book is a collection of the stories that have defined my life and, in doing so, helped me discover meaning in the midst of the mundane.

Life's Gifts

I once had a friend named Fong who immigrated to the United States from China years ago. I am in awe of the courage of immigrants. To leave behind all that is familiar—your family, your home, your language, your roots—to start again in a new country? Unfathomable. I asked her once where she'd gotten such extraordinary courage. She thought for a moment and then admitted, "If I had known how hard it would be, I never would have done it."

And that pretty much sums it up. The experiences that have had the most value in my life are ones I never would have done if I'd known how hard they would be. Giving birth. Writing a book. Speaking all over the country to promote adoption. They are all exhausting. But they are also the most memorable, exhilarating, and satisfying experiences of my life.

The simple truth is that the hardest things I've ever had to do in life were the most rewarding. At the top of that list was traveling to a remote corner of the earth to find the children God meant to be mine. Harder than I could ever have imagined. Scarier than I could have fathomed. Exhausting beyond belief. Rewarding beyond measure.

But life, even at its most trying, is filled with gifts that we only need to be wise enough to see. The gifts are there for all, not just a few. The gifts are meant to give us the strength to get us through the dark moments. They are to be savored. They bring us joy.

Sometimes we miss the gifts that are right in front of us until we're at the end of our lives and we more clearly understand the beginning.

Life is not meant to be a survival of the fittest. Life is not meant to defeat us. Life is not meant to beat us down.

The gifts restore us. They give us hope. They give our lives meaning. They are meant to be savored.

The gifts belong to all of us.

Claim them.

The First Gift

The Past

$\mathcal{S}$ometimes the hardest place to begin is at the beginning. But to understand the ending, you must know the beginning. Who we were in the past is the foundation for who we are now. All of us are the sum total of our experiences, the collage of our unique stories. But while we can deny our past, we can never escape it; what has already happened to us forms the lens through which we see our future. If our past has taught us to see ourselves as victims, we then expect others to take advantage of us. But if we have learned that the world is full of possibilities, we are optimistic at each turn.

Those who have known difficult times may view the past as anything but a gift. They've run from it their whole lives. They've tried desperately to forget it. The past is where mistakes are buried. It is where those deepest regrets are stuffed.

Most people start out in a family, and all families have their share of dysfunction. That's because we're all humans, and any combination of human beings is pretty much a recipe for some type of dysfunction. We hurt each other's feelings. We make each other angry. We fail to meet expectations. We do stupid stuff. We falter. We fall down.

But family is also where we learn to love. To compromise. We try harder. We ask for forgiveness. We rise again. We triumph.

I was one of the lucky ones. I have no need to escape my past. In fact, for nearly all my adult life, I lived within ten miles of the home I grew up in. This is not to say that I escaped hurt scot-free. I had my share of heartbreak and failure. But there was always a generous blend of love and success mixed in as well. I was co-cooned by loving parents and an intact family. They protected me against want, violence, and worry. I always had the safety net of family. And the shield of love.

Maybe this is why I was destined to learn so many lessons from the past of another: enter Jaclyn. She came into my life at a time when I had it all. My family life was nearly perfect. I was married to a successful attorney. We had a beautiful six-year-old daughter, Kate, who amazed and delighted me at every turn. I had the sweetest toddler imaginable, Christy, who officially became my daughter on my first visit to China in 1998. I had a challenging job as an administrator in an urban school district. My home was beautiful. I was in good health. I had a wonderful network of friends. I loved my life. I would have been hard-pressed to even breathe a wish that was not within my power to grant.

A friend once told me that the only right time to add a child to your family is when you're happy and healthy and well-adjusted. So when I saw a precious four-year-old Chinese orphan advertised on the Internet through a "waiting child" list, it seemed the perfect opportunity to add another daughter to the mix.

As I think back to that time now, I realize that my life was full of me and stuff and obligations. Although it felt full at the time, at some level I had lost my way. I was too busy doing instead of living. I was focused on the things that would make me happy instead of the people. My life wasn't really making a difference. And why should it? It was easier staying in the comfort zone.

Jaclyn changed all that. She would not let me be complacent. She had too much to tell me; she had too much to teach me. I thought I was saving her. The truth is—she saved me.

I had fallen in love with Jaclyn's photo and my vision of what she would be like. In 1999, my husband Rick and I crossed the ocean, naively hoping that the child I longed for based on that single picture—the complete stranger who had seized my heart in a manner I can't begin to explain—would accept me. On a cognitive level, I knew this would not happen immediately. I realized that our start as mother and daughter would begin with some angst. But nothing prepared me for the depths of her despair.

Our first meeting was harder than I could have imagined. She recoiled at the sight of my Caucasian face. When I tried to get her to leave with us, Jaclyn planted her sturdy legs and refused to get into the car. No amount of cajoling from the orphanage staff would sway her. Her grief was so profound it rendered her nearly catatonic.

And so we kidnapped her. Rick picked her up and put her in the backseat, draped stiffly across my lap. I knew she was terrified at leaving behind all that was familiar to her. The truth was that I was terrified too, and there was no turning back.

Many people have asked me what's the hardest part of adopting a foreign child. Is it the language barrier? Teaching her how to fit into a family? Indoctrinating her into a new culture? No, none of those. What I worried most about—communicating with her, socializing her, being able to really love her—was small in

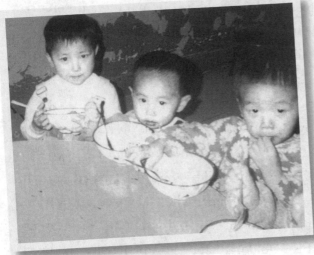
Jaclyn in the orphanage

comparison to the most difficult challenge: listening to her talk of her past.

Unlike most small children, who do everything possible to shut out traumatic memories, Jaclyn came to me with a long list of wrongs. Her past came out in bits and pieces, as she not only struggled to learn a new language but also to make me understand what was incomprehensible. How could a four-year-old child have experienced everything she had?

Her list of hurts was endless:

Hunger. Unending, unrelenting hunger.

Cold. Fingers so cold they were numb, no pajamas, begging for a coat.

The dark. Clasping hands against the demons of the night with other terrified youngsters when the bedroom door was locked in the orphanage at night.

Unspeakable fear. Where would she go next? On what continent would she live? In what kind of living situation? Who would she have to cling to?

Heartbreak. Leaving behind a child she called "her baby," who she had cared for and loved dearly, never knowing if she would ever see him again. Wondering every day if he would survive without her protection.

Abuse. Being beaten with a stick just for talking. Made to stand with arms outstretched until she wanted to scream out in pain. Not being allowed to scream. Crying silent tears.

Owning nothing. Not even having a shelf or a drawer all her own. Having to fight for anything and everything.

Sickness. Lying sideways in a shared hospital bed, hooked up to IVs, having absolutely no idea where she was and why, or how she got there, or if she would ever leave.

Abandonment. The cruelest blow of all. When Jaclyn was two and a half, her mother walked away and left her all alone.

Jaclyn sought understanding. She wanted justice. She demanded to be heard.

Her past was a thief that stole her innocence, her childhood. It nearly stole her life.

But it didn't steal her soul.

She came to me a sturdy warrior, fully capable of caring for herself and others. She needed no one. My job was to teach her how to need someone, preferably me. My job was to teach her how to be a child. Instead, she taught me. The lessons poured forth—profound in their simplicity, staggering in their totality.

Lesson #1: Even a heart that's been broken can love hugely.

On her third day as my daughter, when the shock began to fade and she could find her voice again, Jaclyn told me through our translator that she had a baby. I thought that I had misunderstood.

Knowing a four-year-old couldn't possibly give birth, I asked for details. Jaclyn told me that her job at the orphanage had been to take care of two toddlers. The orphanage housed nearly four hundred children, and due to limited resources, children older than three were expected to help with the younger ones. Jaclyn told us proudly, "Big girls like me can take care of ourselves. So we need to take care of the little ones too."

Jaclyn took good care of Po Po, a little girl, but her heart truly went out to the tiny waif-like boy she nicknamed Xiao Xiao. Her charges shared the bed next to her so she could dress, feed, and wash them. She also protected them from the big kids and comforted them when they were sad. In a world without parents, Jaclyn gave her charges selfless mother love.

It was then that Jaclyn began to negotiate with us. She demanded to take Xiao Xiao with her to her new home. It wasn't possible; we compromised by agreeing that we would take Jaclyn back to the orphanage so she could say goodbye to "her baby."

The minute we entered the room, she pushed through the throng of excited children to claim his hand. She scrutinized his appearance, then gently fixed his pant leg and fussed over his tiny shirt. He was without a doubt the most pitiful child I had ever seen. He looked like a skeleton, with skin stretched tightly over his face. His body was covered in sores, and the hair on his little head was wispy. He clutched Jaclyn's hand as if his life depended on maintaining that grasp.

When we had to go, tears streamed down his face as he said goodbye to the only mother he knew. Jaclyn rocked this child in her embrace, barely a head shorter than she.

This was the most heartbreaking scene I had ever witnessed. But since Jaclyn was so young, I believed she would one day forget her tragic past. I couldn't have been more wrong.

The ghost of Xiao Xiao was everywhere. Jaclyn talked about him daily. She begged every adult she encountered to find him a mama.

Her tenacious advocacy brought about a series of miracles that resulted in these two children being reunited and becoming cousins. Xiao Xiao was adopted by my sister a year after I adopted Jaclyn.[1]

Jaclyn told me she had never seen "her baby" smile when he lived in the orphanage. Now nothing can stop this kid from smiling. He is a joyful, loving, bright, handsome young man who looks nothing like the pitiful creature of long ago.

If Jaclyn can make a difference in the world, so can we.

You don't need money, connections, brilliance, or wonderful communication skills. Jaclyn didn't have any of those things. But we all have at our disposal what she had—fearlessness, persistence, hope, faith, prayer, and love. In the darkest of places, Jaclyn chose love over despair. How can we not do likewise?

When I think back to that time, it's easy to see what Jaclyn didn't have. She didn't have a dime. She didn't have a family. She couldn't read or write. She could barely speak English. She had no power.

She also didn't have fear. Because she didn't know how hard it would be to find a willing adoptive family, she never doubted it would happen for Xiao Xiao.

Her faith in me made me forge ahead without being frozen by the fear that I would fail her. Even when doubt nagged at me, when common sense told me it would never happen, her trust kept me from wavering.

Someone once told me that every child's negative quality has a positive side. Jaclyn's stubbornness was the persistence that enabled her to survive. Her strong will meant she could be intractable—and also that she was not easily dissuaded. This child continually did everything in her power to make her dreams come true.

If we both survive her adolescence, I know Jaclyn will become a woman to be reckoned with. She is capable of using her strong will, her unwavering beliefs, and her tenacious personality to make a difference in this world.

While it's easy to see what Jaclyn didn't have, I've clearly seen many things that she does have.

Jaclyn has hope. Before we knew her, I chose Hope as Jaclyn's middle name. She has proven to be the personification of that word. She clings to hope with both hands. In the orphanage, this radiant little soul did not allow the darkness of her situation to diminish her life-affirming hopefulness. When she left the orphanage, the staff shed tears of sadness over the loss of this bright light in their lives.

Jaclyn has faith—in people and in the future. She has every reason to conclude that the world is an ugly place. But she didn't. She has a zest for life that's contagious. She throws herself into everything she does, truly expecting good things to happen. She trusts. Her soul is intact.

For most people, abandonment would have been the defining moment of their life. They would thereafter refuse to love or to trust, and who would blame them? After all, the wounded seek to hurt others. We think heartbreak happens when we lose our first love, usually our high school boyfriend or girlfriend. But our first love is our mom. When you lose her, the wound is gaping. But Jaclyn discovered the only way to piece together a broken heart. Though she herself did not have a mother's love, she chose to love another. By doing so, she unleashed the most healing, the most powerful force in life.

Lesson #2: Begin with a grateful heart.

I don't know if I was more or less grateful than everyone else; I simply took for granted the abundance in my life. After all, we live in a country where we don't have to think about where our next meal is coming from. We're more inclined to notice that our neighbor has a better car, a nicer house, or more designer shoes than we do. Until we meet someone who has nothing.

Within a few months of Jaclyn's adoption, Christy's sitter, Darla, watched all three of my daughters while I accompanied my husband to a social event at his office. In a clear lapse of sanity, Darla decided to take the girls to a giant toy store and let them each pick out their heart's desire. I understood what motivated Darla—it was hard not to want to indulge Jaclyn.

In the institution, she had nothing to call her own—everything was shared. The child who made it to the pile of clothing first in the morning got the best choice for the day. The latecomer was relegated to a flannel nightgown worn as a dress in 80-degree heat. Oftentimes feet had to be fitted into the only pair of shoes left—which were usually several sizes too small. Jaclyn had no possessions, no shelf, no safe place to store any treasure, however meager, of her own. Her delight in the smallest treat made my heart ache, and Darla had seen this.

When she and the three kids arrived at the store, six-year-old Kate and two-year-old Christy made a mad dash for the Barbie aisle. Jaclyn seized an umbrella. It was gaudy hot pink and covered with feathers.

Puzzled by this choice, Darla tried to gently dissuade her. But Jaclyn was thrilled with it and wouldn't consider anything else. She could hardly wait to show her incredible treasure to me when I picked her up.

I too puzzled over why she had chosen this. Had she noticed people in China using them for sunshields? Was it the ultimate fashion accessory for a child with an unusual sense of style? Did she even know what it was?

"Why did you pick an umbrella, Jaclyn?" I asked.

She replied matter-of-factly: "For raining."

The next morning she ran down the stairs, clutching her umbrella, and raced to the window.

Jaclyn with her umbrella

"Raining?" she asked hopefully. Her expression fell when she saw the glorious sunrise.

Months later, after she had learned the words she needed to make herself understood, the mystery was revealed.

"Mama," she told me, "in China, the window in the room where the kids sleep broken. Rain come in at night. Kids with beds by the window get all wet. In the morning the teachers say the kids peep the bed. But they not! Teachers hit the kids for peep the bed."

No wonder the umbrella had delighted her so. To be protected from the rain—what unspeakable joy!

This was just the first of many glimpses into her past that helped me understand the enormity of the gap between the "haves" in this world and the "have nots." When December came, it triggered her memory of her last winter in China. It had been unusually cold for that region, and the orphanage lacked the warm clothing necessary to protect children who lived in buildings with open windows and no heating system.

"I begged the teacher for a coat because I so cold," Jaclyn remembered with a shiver. "I got a coat, but my fingers still so cold." She rubbed her hands together at the memory. "I so shivering at night. I no have warm jammies, just little shirt and underpants. One blanket. It not enough for one child."

Chastened by the deprivation she had known, I was desperate to try to make it up to her. In a clear lapse of judgment, I planned a trip to Disney World a few months after her adoption. The difficulty of managing three small kids at the Magic Kingdom was compounded by the fact that Jaclyn was still adjusting to everything in her new life.

At one point, as I was trying to get Christy into her stroller, Jaclyn dove head first into a fountain. She could not fathom why so many people had just walked by the plethora of pennies in the water, and she was determined not to make the same mistake.

Later, as we were walking through the park, Kate said, "Mom, Jaclyn's got gum."

Rick and I exchanged puzzled glances; neither of us had given her gum. Suddenly, the light bulb went on. We had just visited the bathroom, where Jaclyn had discovered some used gum on the floor and had popped it into her mouth.

I scolded her sternly and made her throw it out. I felt sure she had understood what I was saying. But the next day, Kate reported again, "Jaclyn's got gum!" I tried to explain that she wasn't to eat food she found on the floor, because it had germs.

Months later she confessed how confusing this had been for her. "When you find food on ground in China, it's your lucky day!" she told me.

I shuddered. I certainly didn't let my children eat food that had fallen on the ground, but Jaclyn was so neat and careful she rarely dropped anything.

"In China, food fall on the floor, other kids grab it. They don't even ask." Then she added, "Sometimes kids grab it while it still in little kid's hand."

I could tell she was thinking of Xiao Xiao. I wondered how often he'd gone hungry because an older child stole food he'd found. "Things are different here," I said.

"I know," she said. "In China, we no have germs!"

I smiled at her rationalization and did not correct her. And I tried to wrap my brain around a world where food left on the ground is prized. I was no longer viewing want from the distance afforded by my TV screen; I now understood it first-hand from its witness.

The lessons continued. As I was doing the breakfast dishes one morning, Jaclyn watched me scrape away the remains from breakfast and shovel pieces of half-eaten toast into the disposal.

"Why people waste food?" she asked.

With a jolt, I realized that my garbage disposal probably ate better than most of the world's children.

She never forgot where she had been and what she had experienced. One day, after I'd bought each of my girls a new pair of tennis shoes, I struggled to lace each pair so the girls could run out to play. I tied Jaclyn's shoes last. I was sure she'd run off after her sisters the minute the bow was tight, but she didn't. Instead, she grabbed my hand, looked into my eyes, and said solemnly, "Thank you, Mama, for new shoes."

Her past had taught her gratitude, and not just about possessions.

When Jaclyn was eight, she overheard me talking to my mother about a dear friend of ours. Al had lost his job unexpectedly. He was worried about the financial devastation to his family. He was likely going to have to relocate. His oldest daughter was getting divorced. The cumulative stress of these events had brought on heart palpitations.

After I hung up, Jaclyn approached me and said, "I know what's wrong with Uncle Al."

I smiled indulgently, waiting for a child's medical diagnosis.

"He's wishing for too many things." And then, in a quieter voice she explained what she meant. "When I lived in China, I only wished for one thing. I wished for a mama. When you wish for too many things, your heart hurts."

I was struck by the intuitiveness of her pronouncement.

I thought of how often we use the phrase "my heart's desire" and follow it with a request for an expensive car, a dazzling piece of jewelry, a new kitchen, a fabulous trip.

What our hearts truly desire is love. And if we have that, our gratitude should begin there. What I learned from Jaclyn's perspective was how much I took for granted. We have to remind ourselves to be grateful; it doesn't happen on a daily basis. When forced during the "around the table" Thanksgiving ritual to say what they are thankful for, many stumble, hoping that the person in front of them doesn't steal their choice. "Health," "home," "family," and "friends" predictably top the list. What about life? When you have known someone who has been abandoned, someone who fought for their survival before they reached school age, you learn that life is not a given. What about having never known hunger? What about protection from the elements? What about just having a mom?

I will likely never have a sports car, a dazzling diamond, or a mini-mansion. And I couldn't care less. Jaclyn has taught me that I have everything that really matters.

Lesson #3: To know who you are and where you came from is a gift.

I never knew when fleeting ghosts from Jaclyn's past might surface next. I'd get lulled into thinking we were finally living in the present, and then one would peek out from its hiding place. Sometimes the reminders of who she was and where she came from empowered her to navigate the present. But other times the memories brought heartache with them and laid it at my feet. Often reminders of her past were like sucker punches; I never saw them coming.

In second grade, Jaclyn's class studied Dr. Martin Luther King. One of her assignments was to complete a grid comparing her life to Dr. King's. Under "Life Goal," she had written for Dr. King, "To make the world a better place." For herself, she wrote, "Lifeguard."

"Lifeguards don't get paid very much," I said in a teasing voice. "You're not going to be able to afford a car that 'blows your hair' or the fancy house you're dreaming of if you become a lifeguard."

"But they save people's lives," Jaclyn said indignantly.

I let this one go. There was plenty of time for her to learn of the inverse relationship between the importance of certain jobs—teacher, nurse, daycare worker—and the pay they received.

Under "Mother's Occupation," she had correctly written that Dr. King's mother was a teacher. Under her mother's occupation, she wrote one word: *babies.*

I was proud of her answer. Though my day job was school administration, advocating for children was my life's work.

She correctly recorded the profession of Dr. King's father. But her own father's occupation she left blank.

"I don't know what Daddy does," she told me.

"I'm a lawyer," Rick replied. "When people have a fight about something, I help make it better."

"Or worse," I mumbled under my breath.

Another column was blank: her date of birth.

"Jaclyn, you know your birth date—October 1, 1997."

Jaclyn fixed her eyes on mine. And then came the punch. "You don't know when my birthday really is."

Instantly, I was back in time, three and a half years earlier, remembering the day we took Jaclyn back to the orphanage to say good-bye to Xiao Xiao. The director told me a beautiful story about how she had picked Jaclyn's birth date. She wanted her to have "the luckiest birthday in China" because she had come to them with one of the saddest stories. I cringed at the memory of her saying that Jaclyn had been "discarded"—and using this horrific term in front of a four-year-old child. It had never been spoken of since.

I'd grown up hearing my mom tell the stories of my birth. I knew how many days late I was, how difficult her labor was, how fatigued my mother was by the time I arrived, what time of day I was born, what I looked like minutes after my birth. I knew all the pieces of who I was.

Jaclyn had none of the pieces of her past.

Suddenly, I was filled with a different perspective on the importance of our beginning. I know some reading this who might say, "I have nothing to be grateful for in my past." Or "my family was dysfunctional." Or "we were poor." Or "I am a child of divorce." I am not minimizing these experiences. They are real hurts. They can cause a protective shell to envelop the heart forever. But think for a moment of this: do you know what your mother's face looks like? Do you know your own birthday? Do you know the place where you were born, where you first were welcomed into the world? The things that we take for granted, the smallest truths about our lives, become huge when they are absent.

A few months later, after watching the TV news report a story about a despicable criminal, Jaclyn asked, "How does someone get so bad?"

The psychologist in me knows that unspeakable behavior often begins with a child no one has claimed, invested in, or loved. And maybe the greatest miracle of all is that Jaclyn did not become one of those damaged beings. Instead, she endured adversity and came out of it wise, grateful, forgiving, and caring.

In understanding where she had been and what she had endured, I was changed by the lessons she brought with her. I now understood her truths:

- Our past is a gift. Without it, we have a hole in our soul defined by the question of who we are.

- We can choose love even when we have been betrayed.

- We can choose joy even when every experience in life has shown us sorrow.

- We can choose hope even in the darkest circumstances.

- We can choose courage even when we have to stare down fear. We don't have to let the demons of the past swallow us.

- We can choose to be grateful. We live in the most privileged nation on earth. Our hearts should be filled with gratitude in proportion to that privilege.

- We can choose to trust. There are bad people in the world. There are also good people who do bad things. But there are good people who do good things too. Jaclyn counted on me to be one of them.

The past is our teacher. Our guide. Sometimes it is even our friend. It shows us what we are capable of—both the good and the bad. It instructs us. It challenges us.

The past gives us roots—some that we try desperately to escape, some that ground us forever. Surviving fire makes metal stronger. So it is with our past. Surviving trials makes us stronger. The past gives us the gifts of resilience, courage, and a reason to believe that we can endure and even triumph.

And for these reasons, the past is the most illuminating gift of life.

[1]The account of Jaclyn's selfless devotion to Xiao Xiao is chronicled in my book *The Waiting Child: How the Faith and Love of One Orphan Saved the Life of Another* (St. Martin's Press, March 2003).

The Second Gift

The Plan

$\mathscr{A}$ few years ago, my good friend George went through a long period of unemployment. I mean *long*. Although he was a skilled negotiator representing management during complex labor negotiations, he had lost this high-paying executive level job due to some ugly internal politics. Checking his anger at the unfairness of it all, he confidently jumped headlong into a job search. He was certain he would find a better position and that things would work out for the best in the end. He made it as a finalist for several great jobs, but each time, the rug was pulled out from under him. Disappointment after disappointment piled up.

Because I am both his friend and a psychologist, I watched for signs of despair. They never surfaced. At each new job interview, he brought genuine enthusiasm to the table. And when things didn't work out as he had hoped, he said with no sign of regret, "Well, I guess it wasn't in the plan."

George saw his newfound idleness as the perfect opportunity to become chief babysitter for his new granddaughter, and she thrived due to his attention.

George also announced to his church that he was available for volunteer service and willing to help wherever they needed it. When he was asked to lead the singing at a nursing home, he didn't back away. This six-foot-three, 225-pound former University of

Michigan football player who can't carry a tune in a basket enthusiastically directed a choir of nodding-off, wheelchair-bound seniors. Being faithful in this task got him promoted to a volunteer position working as a support counselor at an in-patient substance-abuse center for men. He found this opportunity so rewarding, he wondered if this might be his destined path.

His job search went on for nearly two years. His savings disappeared. His house was on the brink of foreclosure. And still, he remained sanguine.

George finally ended up with a great job in the most unlikely place—working for the union he had formerly bargained against. It was the last place he thought he would end up, yet it was the perfect fit.

Inspired by his example, I asked him how he was able to remain so positive, so sure that everything would turn out okay with nothing to support that belief. Without hesitation, he answered, "I believe in a God who has a plan for each of our lives. A plan for our ultimate good. When you truly believe that in your heart, you can let go of all the worry in life. If something doesn't work out for you, it's because *it's not in your plan.*"

This is a hard concept for me, because I like to be in control. I need to know what's next. Life has to make logical sense to me. But if I step back and think of God's bigger picture, why would I want to mess with His plan? My vision of the future is cloudy at best. The One who holds the plan holds all knowledge too.

Believe in the plan. Believe in the One who knows the plan.

Life is not a series of random events strung together by luck.

I've been asked many times what first got me interested in international adoption. I was not the typical candidate. I wasn't infertile. I already had one child—a precious daughter, Kate— which fulfilled my biological ticking-clock desires for mother- hood. I had never planned on having more than one child. And I was beyond the age when most people are considering more children.

Then one cold December evening when Kate was a little over two, she came to me as I was hunkered down in bed reading and said very matter-of-factly, "My baby sister is coming pretty soon!"

I was more than a little surprised. We had never discussed hav- ing another child, and she had never mentioned having a sibling. She was a solitary child who had learned to entertain herself easily, and she seemed content with the quiet cadence of our life.

I gave her a patronizing smile and shook my head "no." She gave me a patronizing smile back and nodded her head "yes." Curiosity got the better of me, and I wondered who had put her up to this.

"Did someone tell you to say that to me?" I asked gently, hop- ing to ID the culprit and straighten him or her out.

"Yes."

"Who?"

"An angel," she whispered.

I gave her another patronizing smile. Little kids get confused all the time. I dismissed it as a reaction to watching too many holiday specials on TV.

That summer, Oprah aired a show with secret film footage taken inside Chinese orphanages. The documentary was called "The Dying Rooms," and I found it nearly impossible to watch.

Like everyone else, I'd seen plenty of tragic happenings on TV. Every day the evening news portrayed all kinds of horrors suffered by children who live outside the protection of families. I usually tried to forget about it when the program ended.

But the crying of those dying babies in China reverberated inside me. I could not shake the memory of their hopeless eyes. Something had to be done.

I got on the Internet and searched for organizations I could make a donation to. After all, money eases conscience, and this seemed the most expedient solution. But searching the web drew me in as I read more and more about the desperate situation of the orphans in China. Interspersed with these accounts were compelling first-person stories about brave American parents who ventured into China and adopted these orphans, bringing them to new lives in the United States.

International adoption struck me as crazy, dangerous, illogical, and frightening. But over time, reading stories of families who had successfully navigated a shaky adoption program made me want to become part of the solution. It was my chance to do some small thing with my life to give back. I wanted in.

I had no idea where to begin. Who can you trust to find you a baby in a foreign country? I ended up putting my faith in a woman named Snow who had recently emigrated from China with a determination to find families for as many Chinese orphans as she could. She knew nothing of our convoluted immigration system, how to start up a business, how to market, or even where to begin. Within five years, she was running one of the largest China adoption agencies in the world. Yet each family and each child was special to her.

Even so, for a logical, pragmatic lady like me to trust my future to a woman in Texas I'd never met was a huge step of faith. And one that proved to be amazingly fortuitous.

The next step was to put together a dossier of voluminous paperwork that would be sent to China as evidence of my worthiness to parent. I could write a whole book on what that entailed, but suffice it to say that the rules were evolving at that time. I had to pull in a lot of favors to get a secret phone number at INS so I could speak to an actual human being. There were more security checks, health exams, screenings, social-work visits, and disclosures than NASA requires to enter the space program.

Oh, did I mention that I also had to obtain an original certified, notarized, sealed copy of my marriage license? And that was made incredibly more challenging due to the fact that I had eloped on a Caribbean island, and the original marriage license had been housed in a building that had been destroyed by a hurricane.

I nearly gave up on more than one occasion. And I quickly learned that breaking into hysterical tears was the only way to get bureaucrats to do anything to help.

Being the practical person I am, I requested a three-year-old daughter so Kate would have a sibling close to her age. When I told Kate that her new sister would be a "big girl" like her, she looked at me incredulously and explained, very slowly this time, that her new sister would be a baby.

We then went through the daunting process of an adoption home study, in which every detail of our life was scrutinized and evaluated. Naturally, we were anxious to present our family in the best possible light. So I left out a few somewhat embarrassing but seemingly irrelevant details—for instance, that my stepdaughter, Julie, was married to Tom Arnold. Yes, the one of Roseanne fame.

Our beautiful, sweet, twenty-one-year-old college coed had met him while visiting her brother in California. She quickly became enthralled with Hollywood; they were married within the year. My faith teaches that everything works together for good, but it was hard for me to find the good in this. The Hollywood lifestyle, fraught with risks and heartache, was not the future we had imagined for her.

When we filled out our adoption application, I glossed over this embarrassing little fact by indicating that our son-in-law was "in the entertainment business." I figured Snow was new to the US and likely didn't even know who Tom Arnold was.

After the dossier was filed in China in October 1996, I began the anxious wait for news of my child. In spite of Kate's prediction of a baby, I reserved a spot for my new daughter at Kate's Montessori school, expecting to travel to China in the next few weeks to bring her home. Our family would surely be complete by Christmas.

And then the worst possible news came—the Chinese government, overwhelmed by a flood of new interest, decided to close the adoption program for review. A black curtain descended. For weeks, we heard no news. Not even any indication of when there would be news. We had no reason to believe the adoption program would ever start up again. I sank into despair.

As the weeks dragged on, I was desperate for support. Every person I knew became sick to death of hearing me whine about it. I wasn't going to make it without a hand to hold. Correction—a hand to desperately clutch.

The Internet, my main source of information on international adoption, brought me to an unlikely support group. Other desperate parents had formed a Yahoo group for all of us who had our hearts committed to a Chinese adoption and our lives on hold awaiting any new developments. Literally overnight, thousands of prospective parents from all over the world joined the group to share the latest rumors, discuss their fears, and second-guess everything, including ourselves. I followed those daily digests frantically. On some days, they were the only thing that got me out of bed.

One day an e-mail was posted by a woman named Donna. She indicated in her signature line that she was hoping to be matched to an older orphan—one between the ages of three and five. On a whim, I e-mailed her directly, mentioning that I too had asked for an older child. A friendly response followed, and a cyber friendship quickly grew.

As we shared more about ourselves, the similarities were eerie. We were both blondes of about the same age with biological kids and a desire to change the world one child at a time. We had even chosen the same adoption agency. We had similar religious beliefs, similar challenges balancing work and family, and were both addicted to M&M candies. Donna lived in Texas, a state I had never visited. I lived in Michigan, a state she had never visited.

Donna knew just what to say to me on my dark days and never failed to reassure me that our daughters were out there waiting for us. She held my hand through cyberspace.

Unlike me, Donna never lost hope. Likely fed up with my despair, she finally confronted me point-blank, in the direct way that e-mail allows and asked: "How big is your God?" Confused by the question, I hesitated. She then wrote: "If you believe in a God that created the heavens and the earth in a single week, couldn't that same God bring two little girls home safely from China? And if God is big enough to accomplish this, why is it so hard for you to have faith?"

Why indeed?

Though Donna and I had never even spoken on the phone, she became my closest confidant. As the months passed and our e-mail bond grew, we began to correspond about the possibility of a visit. After seven months of daily exchanges, she flew to Michigan with her daughter to meet Kate and me. I recognized her immediately when she got off the plane; she was instantly familiar, and we spent a long weekend talking endlessly.

On multiple occasions we mused about how amazing it would be if we were able to travel to China together to bring our daughters home, but we scoffed at the improbability of it. There were thousands of orphanages all over China, housing hundreds of thousands of orphans. Our paperwork had not even gone to China at the same time. Really, what would be the odds?

As I waited for my new child, I frantically searched the Internet for any information on China adoption and scoured every website I could find on the topic. One of those was a site titled "Rainbow Kids." It contained adoption-related articles and links as well as a list of international "waiting children"—those who were considered hard to place due to age or special needs.

One night, as I perused the waiting children listing, a photo leaped out at me. It was child #35, a three-year-old Chinese orphan wearing a forlorn expression and a green coat. When I looked at that picture, I knew with certainty that I had never known before that she was destined to be my daughter.

The next day I contacted the adoption agency that held her file and explained that I already had a dossier in China, and I recognized child #35 as my daughter, and would they please make the match for me so I could bring her home? The adoption agent hemmed and hawed. Although most agencies are manned by loving staff members with generous hearts, this one seemed more concerned about their inability to collect any fees from me, since my dossier had been filed through another agency.

The agent said she would call me back. Two days later I got a call stating that one of *their* families was going to adopt child #35. She politely thanked me for my interest and hung up.

More than a little surprised, I vowed to pray daily for child #35 and never forget her. I never did. Since I didn't know her name, I dubbed her "the little girl in the green coat" in my prayers.

As the months dragged on and we neared the one-year mark since our dossier had been sent to China, my daily correspondence with Donna saved my sanity.

One day I was glancing at the calendar and felt a strong premonition. Now, I'd like to mention in this part of the story that I'm not a witch or anything. For those who have never had a premonition, it feels like a really strong hunch that made no sense at the time. I've had a few of them in my life; all have been accurate. They come from the Holy Spirit. I immediately e-mailed Donna and told her that I knew with certainty she would have some news of her child on Friday, November 7. She didn't question the logic of this pronouncement at all.

Donna and I and our long-awaited babies on the day of their adoptions in China

On Friday, November 7, she was scheduled to volunteer at her daughter's school. That morning she decided to remain at home, explaining to her husband Mike that she needed to stay close to the phone because I had told her "the call" was coming that day and she didn't want to risk missing it. (These were the days before cell phones.)

Mike looked at her like she was nuts. "Just because Cindy says it doesn't mean it's true," he chided her. He encouraged her to go to the school. She left with more than a little reluctance.

At 8:45 that morning, my phone at work rang. It was the adoption agency, informing me that my future daughter—a four-month-old infant—was waiting for me in a tiny remote town in China. Shocked and excited, I couldn't wait to share the news. My husband was traveling and unreachable. With shaking fingers, I dialed Donna's number. Mike answered the phone.

As I breathlessly told him the tidbits of information I had about my baby, call waiting went off on his end. Apologizing profusely, he said he had to put me on hold as he was an on-call pilot for a major airline. I waited, but he never came back on the line. I finally hung up.

Minutes later he called me back. The interruption had not been the airline; it was "the call." He had needed a few minutes to compose himself because of the incredible news: they had a four-month-old infant daughter waiting for them in China. In the same orphanage, in the same tiny town, as my baby girl.

Two months later, Donna and I boarded a long series of flights that took us to a rural village in China. The orphanage there had only done five adoptions prior to ours, and no one traveling in our group of adoptive families had babies in the same city. Donna and I were alone but together in navigating the paths of this strange and wondrous adventure.

When we got to the orphanage, we discovered that our daughters had been snuggled together sharing one crib during all those months that we had held hands through cyberspace.

As we rode in the bus back to our hotel, clutching our precious babies, I asked Donna, "What are the odds of the two of us finding each other in a cyber support group that had thousands of families from all over the world, and then finding out our babies are crib mates?"

She grinned at me. "God knew our babies were together. So He helped us find each other. It was all part of His plan."

Christy was not the older child I had dreamed of; she was a baby who brought me joy beyond my wildest dreams.

"The plan" helps us discover the people who are our destiny; there are no coincidences.

Everyone I knew was as surprised as I was to find that we were not matched to a three-year-old toddler, as we had requested, but to an infant. Everyone but Kate.

And her angel.

> ## "All things work together for good to them that love God" (Romans 8:28).

I've never before told the story of how Jaclyn came to be my daughter. Maybe I feared the consequences for those who circumvented the system to make her homecoming a reality. Maybe I feared no one would believe the incredible sequence of circumstances that had to all fall together perfectly for it to happen. The time to tell her story is now.

I returned home in January of 1998 with my precious baby, Christy, eager to resume my old life. Little did I realize that my old life was over.

The Chinese have an expression that I love: "The journey of discovery comes not from seeing new lands but from seeing with new eyes." And that was how it was for me. Once I had been inside a third-world orphanage, once I had looked into the eyes of despair, once I had touched the hands of want, the world looked completely different to me.

Whenever I surveyed the racks of shoes in my closet, I'd flash back to the orphans I had seen walking barefoot on a cold January morning. When I'd go shopping and see someone purchasing a coat for her dog, I had to hold myself back from grabbing it out of her hands and screaming, "Don't you realize that there are *kids* in this world who have no coats?"

I had become someone new, with a new awareness of the privilege of my place in this world. I could never forget what I had seen or go back to who I had been.

Every day I had a nagging sense that I was meant to do more. But what? I thought more and more about child #35, the little girl in the green coat. Surely she must be with her adoptive family by now.

I picked up the phone and called the adoption agency that had held her file and begged them for news of how she was doing. A long silence. And then I heard the words that nearly stopped my heart: she'd had not one but two adoptions fall through. Each time her file had been matched to a family, the adoption had been stopped due to "a problem." The agent didn't know what the issue was but thought it might be a medical problem. Each adoptive family had been matched to a different child instead. After child #35 was "rejected" twice, she had been dropped from the adoption program. Have a good day. Click.

I was incensed by this cavalier explanation; these children were not interchangeable commodities. Child #35 would never be adopted. It was unthinkable! I sprang into action.

I first called my husband, Rick. "We are not going back to China," he said firmly. "Don't even think about it."

Not dissuaded, I called the woman who had facilitated Christy's adoption.

Snow answered my call immediately and, before I could say anything, she began to apologize profusely. She assumed I was calling to complain about Christy's poor medical prognosis. Shortly after arriving home from China, medical tests had revealed that Christy had liver disease. I had purposefully not told this to Snow because I didn't want her to think I was anything but joyful over my new baby. Unbeknownst to me, another adoptive family had told her. I shook off Snow's apology and assured her that I had won the lottery. Christy was the sweetest baby imaginable, and I didn't for a minute regret adopting her or wish for another child.

It was not my intent to leverage Snow's guilt for a favor, she owed me nothing, but I did want her help. But Snow, a very proud woman from a culture that values "saving face" above all else, wanted desperately to somehow make amends for placing a seriously ill child in my family. She listened attentively to my sad saga about child #35. She heard in my voice the determination I felt to save her from a future with no hope. Then she gave me a reality check. "My agency doesn't hold her file. Files are confidential. I can't get it to see what the problem is. It would be like me walking into your US social security office and demanding to see a file that wasn't mine. It isn't possible. I'm sorry." Click.

Every shred of logic in me said to let it go. Rick had said no. Snow had said no. But my heart wouldn't say no.

I begged my husband to call the adoption agency that held child #35's file. Maybe there was a way to sponsor her or provide support for her. My tactic worked.

After a phone call with the same cavalier agent I had talked to, Rick became equally incensed at what had happened to this child. How could they not know what had happened? How could they not care? Although he never said we would try to adopt her, I knew he was in.

Now there was just Snow. I continued to call her. She continued to graciously accept my calls but was no less firm in her response. Maybe she was testing my tenacity. Maybe she was waiting, as I was, for divine inspiration.

Months passed, and a terrible flood occurred in China. This gave me an idea. I knew the Chinese looked favorably on people who offered "gifts" when asking for government services. I called Snow and asked if she thought a donation toward flood relief might convince the officials to let someone view the file of child #35 to determine if she could be adopted.

Jaclyn's picture as child #35 on the Rainbow Kids list wearing her green coat

Snow sighed deeply and then admitted that she'd been wrack-
ing her brain for ideas on how to approach this. And then she
busted me by revealing that she had known all along what I had
tried to hide during the home study process: "I know your family is related to actor Tom Arnold. His movie *True Lies* was recently released in China and has become tremendously popular.
The Chinese love American movie stars. If you could get him to
contact some Chinese officials on your family's behalf, offering
autographed pictures as proof of your connection, that might be
enough for child #35's file to be released."

Finally, a plan. A desperate long shot, but a plan nonetheless.
After I hung up, I wondered how Snow found out about our connection to this particular celebrity.

Tom could not have been more accommodating. In fact, he
and Julie had recently done some fundraising for then-President
Clinton, so he generously offered autographed pictures of them
arm-in-arm with the president. A heartfelt letter went with it,
containing a plea for this child's life.

I mailed the letter and pictures to Snow and waited.

Without telling me, for fear of my crushing disappointment
if she failed, Snow flew to Beijing and presented these pleas to
the officials in person.

When she returned to the US, she called me breathless. "Get
a dossier done as quickly as possible. Child #35's file is hidden in
an official's desk drawer, waiting to be matched to *you*."

All that had been wrong with her paperwork was that her
physical form was missing. Snow had hired someone to take her

to the doctor for the required exam and then had the paperwork express-mailed from the orphanage to the officials.

Oh, did I mention that Snow never asked me for a dime of reimbursement or compensation for her extraordinary efforts?

It isn't lost on me that in the US, you couldn't trade an auto-graphed picture of Tom Arnold for an ice cream cone. But Snow traded it for Jaclyn's life.

Our dossier was completed in record time. Eight weeks later, Rick and I flew to China to bring her home. She was my child. She was always destined to be my child.

But if I had been matched to Jaclyn when my first dossier was in China, I would never have known the joy of having Christy as my daughter.

If my stepdaughter hadn't married Tom Arnold, we wouldn't have had the connections.

If Christy had not been so seriously ill, Snow might not have been so motivated to help.

If someone hadn't told my secret about being related to Tom Arnold, Snow wouldn't have thought of the strategy that ended up being the key to releasing Jaclyn's file.

If Jaclyn hadn't had two adoptions fall through, she would not have become my daughter. And if she had not found a mother who would tell her story in book form, hundreds of kids wouldn't have found their forever families.

All of the events that seem so tragic individually, worked to-gether to form a magnificent plan that touched lives in ways be-yond our imagination.

Everything works together for good.

Our hands aren't big enough to hold the clock.

One Saturday morning when Jaclyn was about six, she was, as usual, full of questions. She followed me into the bedroom as I began to dress. "Why Christy not have a pacifier when she a baby?"

"They didn't have pacifiers in Christy's orphanage, so she didn't like them. Did they have pacifiers in your orphanage?" Jaclyn's bedroom in the orphanage was on the same hall as the baby nursery. She had told me that the kids were supposed to stay out of the nursery but that she would peek into the windows as they passed by to go down the stairs.

Jaclyn shook her head and then explained, "The mamas bring the pacifiers. They give to the babies."

This was the first time I had heard her directly reference her awareness of the infant adoptions. I ventured into this new area tentatively. "Did you used to see the mamas when they came?"

She nodded. "Sometimes they get a big kid, but mostly they get the babies."

"How did that make you feel?" I asked with a now familiar ache in my gut.

"I feel happy when I see the mamas come. I happy for the babies to get mamas." Then she stopped, pausing to think back about that time. She finally added, "I not sad, because I no want those mamas. I was waiting for *you*."

My heart melted. Her sureness that the mom who was meant for her would eventually come was touching. How could she have been so certain when there was not one hopeful sign, when she had waited so long?

Waiting is high on the list of "Things I Stink At." When I want something, I want it now. It's hard for me to believe that there is any virtue in patience. But what I have come to realize is that it is not just a matter of the right events occurring that make things work out in our lives, but also the sequence and timing of those events. In order for the plan to unfold perfectly, it can't follow our timetable.

If I had been immediately matched to a baby in China when I filed my first dossier, the timing I had hoped and wished and desperately prayed for, Christy would not have been my daughter—she wasn't even born then. And if China had not closed the adoption program for a year, I would not have been frantically searching the Internet for updates and discovered the picture of my waiting child, Jaclyn. If Jaclyn hadn't had to wait so long to find a family—if one of the first two adoption attempts had succeeded—she never would have met her precious baby, Xiao Xiao. He arrived at the orphanage a few days after Jaclyn's second attempted adoption fell through, desperately needing love. That desperate need to be loved was met by one desperate to love. And that love led to Jaclyn's relentless advocacy; without it, he would never have become part of our extended family. The thought of that loss is too painful to even fathom. Hardest to admit of all is this truth: if Jaclyn had not lived so long in the orphanage, she might not have been so determined never to forget those left behind.

I've learned that when I stop watching the sweep of the minute hand, stop frantically fixing my eyes on the calendar, when I lay down the despair that things I want will never happen, they come together in a way that is breathlessly perfect—a way that only made sense all along to the One who holds time in His hands. In time, the perfection of the plan will be revealed; all we have to do is wait.

The most magnificent stained-glass window began with a pile of broken glass.

I was once fortunate enough to work as a school administrator at one of the most prestigious private school systems in the United States. The grounds and the gardens were so awe-inspiring that people had to pay admission to tour them. As I moved between the various schools and museums that covered this wooded, 360-acre campus, I often put the top down on my little red convertible and relished the statues, the fountains, and the sheer lunacy of the beauty of this campus. The renovated mansion that held the executive offices was only open to the public a few times a year, and those tickets were sought after. My office had windows overlooking a sunken garden so spectacular that having coffee while gazing outside never failed to make me catch my breath. No place is utopia, but this place was pretty close.

I had a boss I liked and respected. Over time, I built a fabulous staff. Our student body was international in scope. They amazed and delighted me with their keen intellect and confidence. My job was to help kids who had every advantage have even more advantages.

And yet I was secretly miserable. My conscience nagged at me, even when I willed it to be quiet. I had only one career, just one chance to make a difference with my life. Why had I chosen such an easy course?

After my second year there, a school administrator job opened up at an urban public school district. It was only about ten miles south of the school where I worked, but it was an entirely different world. This school district was on the brink of financial disaster. The majority of the students were at risk—at risk of failing, dropping out, being left behind. Many of them were the children of addicts, of high school drop-outs, of unwed teenage moms, of unemployed and underemployed parents too desperate to survive to invest time in supporting the neighborhood schools. The hallways of the high school were filled not only with the kids the system had failed but also with violence, drugs, and a new generation of teen moms.

When I walked in for the job interview, I knew in my gut that this was my chance to help kids who had no advantages by becoming their advocate. When the position was offered to me, I signed on without a second thought.

Figuring that I'd come to my senses after a few months of this folly, my former boss called me four months into the new job and asked if I was ready to come back. He added the sweetener that this time I'd be a full vice president. With a nice raise. Maybe even a fancy car. All I had to do was say yes.

I said no. It wasn't even hard. I was determined to make a difference.

In this job I met a little dynamo of a woman named Mary Marlan. She'd signed on for the thankless job of being superintendent of an urban school district teetering on the verge of bankruptcy.

She carefully selected as her deputy superintendent a man of character and integrity named Al. I came to admire them both and considered them my friends as well as my colleagues.

Mary too had left an enviable position in a suburban school district to tackle the challenges that loomed Goliath-like before her. A leader like no other, she was filled with optimism in the most dismal circumstances, creative and brilliant, and had a deep love for the children she served. She spent one day a week in the schools, committed to getting to know personally both students and teachers.

But this community was segregated by inequality. A pocket of high-income families, predominantly white, held the power on the school board. The "have nots"—most of them families of color—had endured years of disparate treatment. While white, upper-class children had the best teachers, the best facilities, and the best resources, the children from "have not" families shared textbooks and desks, and had a school with a leaky roof and an erratic heating system.

Mary refused to be brow-beaten into doing things that were wrong, even if the school board saw no reason to change the way things had always been. She would not be silent. This dervish of energy sprang into action. Her dedication cost her everything: her job, her confidence, her passion, her joy, her pride.

The hard things in life can teach us lessons—like how to be resilient. But the lesson I learned was that courage has consequences—and not always good ones.

The day that board fired her, I felt like throwing down my keys and walking out the door with her. Everything inside me told me it was the right thing to do. But I didn't. For two primary reasons:

1. Basically I'm a chicken.
2. I like to eat.

That cowardice came with a price. I beat myself up over it more times than I can count. And a few weeks later, that school board decided they didn't need Al or me, either. Even without us standing up, they knew what team we were on.

In hindsight, I can see that termination as a good thing. But it sure didn't feel like it at the time. As I scrambled to get another job, I was angry. Angry that I had given so much of myself to other people's kids while sacrificing time with my own. Angry that all my hard work was for nothing. Angry that I had given up so much for a swift kick in the pants. I was even angry at God.

I called my best friend, Deb, with the question that gnawed at my soul: "Why did God let something really bad happen to me when I sacrificed so much to come here?" I had done a selfless thing. My intentions were good. I had chosen something hard over something easy. I had sacrificed. We should be rewarded for sacrificing, for doing the right thing, for trying hard to make a difference. It wasn't supposed to end up like this.

Deb thought for a moment and then replied, "Maybe it isn't about the job at all. Maybe God brought you to that place because there's a person there who will make a real difference in your life."

I scoffed and quickly hung up. Poor me.

Now that Al and I were no longer colleagues, my friendship with him expanded to his wife, Sandy. She offered to babysit my girls and even invited them for an extended visit to her cottage that summer. As she grew to love them, she realized she was not ready to be done parenting. She wanted a daughter from China too.

Al adamantly refused. He had been a champion naysayer when I adopted my girls, explaining to me all the reasons it made no logical sense, pointing out that the youngest of his four children had finally started college and freedom was just ahead for him and Sandy.

But Al hadn't counted on the way his heart would be changed through knowing my daughters. Over time, seeing the joy that these little ones brought, his heart softened.

The next summer Al and Sandy brought home from China the sweetest toddler imaginable, Katelyn. Two years later, they returned to China and brought home Katelyn's new sister. They named her Elizabeth, which means appropriately enough "God's promise."

During their scary, complex, bewildering international adoption adventure, Al's lack of support for my adoption came back to him and Sandy in spades through the nay-saying of their best friends. Jack and Melinda told them that what they were doing made no logical sense. They pointed out that they would soon be free as birds, as their youngest son was now a teen.

But Jack and Melinda had not counted on the way their hearts would be changed by knowing Katelyn and Elizabeth. The next summer, they traveled to China and returned home with their new toddler son, T.J.

Every time I see one of those little ones, I know that what I went through at that horrible job pales in comparison to the part I played in linking those precious children to their families . . . and to mine. The plan did not lead to the kind of success I had hoped to make for those urban kids. Instead, it led to something beyond anything I could ever have imagined. I failed miserably at what I hoped to accomplish . . . and succeeded mightily at something much better.

~~~~~

Think of your life as a parade. You march along, hoping to remain in step with all the others, seeing only what is directly before you, with occasional stolen glimpses at what lies behind. You can't see around the next corner. You can't see who will cheer you on next. But looking down from above, God sees the entire parade route. Where we started. Where we will finally finish. And all the steps in between. We see in part; God sees the whole. It's no wonder we have such trouble connecting the dots and understanding how all the seemingly random events work together to make up the parade that is our life. God must chuckle when we finally get it.

The plan will always bring you to the place you were meant to be . . . sometimes with a few lessons learned along the way. But when you drop the burden of figuring it all out on your own and just wait for the next road sign, you free yourself from worry. We are not meant to live like timid mice, frantically trying to find our way around a maze filled with road blocks. We are meant to live as explorers on an adventure, trusting in the One who holds the map.

That's why "the plan" is the most reassuring gift in life.

The Third Gift

Perfect Moments

Years ago I got a small promotion at work. As I did with all good news, I told my mom in a nanosecond. She has always been my biggest cheerleader and the only person I could shamelessly brag to who not only enjoyed it but also buoyed me even further with her profuse enthusiasm.

"What are you going to do to celebrate?" she asked.

I told her I was too busy to even think about celebrating. I had to pick up my three girls from three different schools, make dinner, help with homework, make sure my kids took their baths, get them ready for bed, say prayers with them, and then tackle the dishes and the laundry.

After listening to this endless litany of to-dos, my mom thoughtfully said, "We spend a lot of time on things that are tragic or sad. Visiting loved ones in hospitals. Worrying about tomorrow. Watching helplessly the most recent disaster on the news. Don't you think, when something good happens, we should take the time to celebrate?"

She was right. I viewed celebrating as one more thing to put on my to-do list. I saved it for milestones like the kids' birthdays or family weddings. I rarely celebrated anything that had to do with me. "Me" somehow got lost when I became a mom.

My mother was right. Not only do we forget to celebrate the good stuff, we forget to look for it—to celebrate the moments when, for just one brief second, life comes together in small ways that can, if we pause, leave us breathless. These moments aren't marked by Hallmark cards, and they don't fall on a prescribed day. They are buried in the busyness of everyday life.

It has taken me years to recognize perfect moments when they fall into my lap. But they are meant to be seized. Prized above all. Because perfect moments are true gifts of life.

In an imperfect life, cherish perfect moments.

Shortly after my husband and I adopted Jaclyn, I decided to schedule a professional photo session. Our family was finally complete, and I wanted to announce that news with a perfect family picture Christmas card.

One of my biggest challenges was to find a way to hide four-year-old Jaclyn's self-inflicted new hairdo. Jealous at being left out while I trimmed her sister's bangs, Jaclyn had grabbed the scissors and cut a wide V in the front of her hair. I hadn't thought anything could look worse that her orphanage haircut; I was wrong. I purchased a huge hair bow that disguised most of the damage.

At breakfast, I reminded all family members that their cooperation was required to get us to our appointment by 6:30 sharp.

After rushing home from work that night, I put two-year-old Christy on the potty. After depositing about a quarter of an ounce of tinkle, she leapt up and began the "potty dance." For those who have not had the joy of toilet training a toddler, it goes like this—at the slightest indicator of success, you bound down the hallway, naked, dancing, and screaming, "Potty!" The point of this is so admirers can come and see what you did. The dance is best performed if a frantic adult is chasing you.

Christy performed this ritual with such vigor that she spun herself into a door and banged her eye. A torrent of tears ensued. The eye swelled and reddened. So did her tear-streaked face. I put a cold washcloth on the eye, hoped it wouldn't be too noticeable in the picture, and tried to console her so she'd stop crying.

Meanwhile, the older two had begun a game of "underwear toss." To the uninitiated, it is played like this: each sister tried to outdo the other in flinging their panties onto various objects in the living room. They laughed uproariously when the panties landed on something, challenging each other to outdo that toss. Extra points were awarded for hitting Mommy's crystal vase and living to tell about it.

I was too harried to retrieve the tossed underpants, so I found new ones and wrestled the girls into fancy party slips. This brought on a round of "slip ballerina." In this game, you run as fast as you can away from Mom and dance like a ballerina, making your slip twirl. Extra points are given for making yourself so dizzy that you fall down. I believe the point of the game is to resist getting the dress on for as long as possible.

I caught Kate, Jaclyn, and Christy, one at a time, and tried to put their party dresses on them. This process was aided by helpful comments like "I hate this dress. I look like a dork in it!" and "I want to wear the green dress!" and "Why does she have long sleeves while I have short sleeves?" And my favorite, "Mom, are you wearing *that*?"

With the girls finally dressed, we went downstairs to tackle hair styling. On the way down, someone threw a backpack from the landing and hit Christy in her good eye. She howled again. Oh well, I reasoned, at least her eyes will match.

I forced Kate to let me fix her hair so her prominent cowlick would not appear in this photo, as it had for her school picture. The hair bow went over Jaclyn's hacked-off bangs. Pigtails went into Christy's hair. Jaclyn yanked the bow out of her hair. Christy yanked out her pigtails.

Okay, I told myself. I'll fix their hair when we get there.

I turned around and noticed that Kate had doused her head with water and hair gel. It looked like an oil slick had landed on her. I scolded her. She cried. She pouted, saying her hair looked dumb. I pulled a brush through my own hair, not really caring what I looked like.

When we finally got downstairs, my husband drummed his fingers on the kitchen counter and asked, "What took so long?"

I did not kill him.

We got in the car. We backed down the driveway, and the garage door went down. Then I realized I'd forgotten the cast-off hair bows. The car went back up the driveway. The garage door went up. I got the bows and returned to the front passenger seat. We backed down the driveway, and the garage door went down. I'd forgotten the checkbook. The car went back up the driveway. The garage door went back up. I got out. I got back in the car with the checkbook. I was already exhausted.

On the way to the photographer's, I noticed three stains on my white jacket. Likely splashed grape juice. I didn't care. I was determined to have my perfect family picture, no matter what.

The first photo of Jaclyn was taken before I adopted her. A woman at the orphanage had told me about that day.

"A very shy and quiet little girl timidly came forward upon her teacher's instruction. She walked with her head down, never looking up. When she got to me, I reached out to embrace her. She looked at her teacher for permission before she dared to hug me back."

It was hard to believe that this description was of the same child that I knew. Full of exuberant energy, she was nearly impossible to subdue.

"When she was told I wanted to take her picture, she lit up like a Christmas tree." Jaclyn understood the connection between having her picture taken and "finding a mama."

"After the picture was taken, she winked at me, then returned to her seat, head bowed as if the weight of the world were on her shoulders. The aura of sadness about her was so profound that it was all I could do not to grab her and take her home with me."

I've seen the picture she took that day. Though it's unmistakably my Jaclyn, the child in that photo bears little resemblance to the child she is today. I cannot even imagine what had been done to her to make the joyful child I now know into that somber being.

I was determined to get a perfect picture of our family that reflected the joy I saw in all of us.

We finally arrived at the photographer's home studio. As we stepped into the bright light, my husband said, "What is that all over your jacket?"

I ignored him.

The photographer's wife/assistant oohed and aahed over how adorable the girls were. Then Jaclyn spotted their cat and tried to step on it. Jaclyn had never seen pets when she lived in China; her only exposure to small animals was mice and rats. The photographer's wife didn't know this and was not amused.

While the photographer set up his camera, the kids fidgeted. I wanted to implore him to hurry before someone started to lose it. Like me.

He tried to set up elaborate poses. But Jaclyn decided she didn't want her picture taken. Assuming my saccharine sweet, public mommy voice, I said, "Come on, sweetie. Just one picture. You look so pretty!"

Jaclyn pouted. The photographer started to sweat.

My husband said, "Let me hold her." This was a façade for getting close enough to hiss in Jaclyn's ear, "Do you want to go in the time-out chair?"

She whined.

We chided her behind clenched smiles and finally got in a few shots.

The photographer decided to try props. He brought out a beautiful, white Victorian baby carriage. Jaclyn loved it. She pushed it around with such fury the wheels shook. So did the photographer.

He then made a fatal error—he showed the kids where all the toys and props were hidden. They descended like a swarm of locusts. Six little hands grabbed toys and flung them to the floor as fast as they could.

I tried to put them away, but the kids kept taking them out. I had a fleeting memory of the old *I Love Lucy* episode where Lucy is on the candy assembly line and the chocolates keep coming faster and faster, and she can't keep up.

After an hour, the photographer firmly bid us goodbye. He was done. I was done. We were all done. I corralled the kids and strode out the door. Every muscle ached with the strain of trying to create this perfect picture.

Outside, dusk had turned to night. Jaclyn, who had lived for so long in an orphanage where bedtime was marked by dusk, whose only glimpse of the night sky had been through a broken window while locked in a room with a dozen other terrified children— exuberantly ran out into the yard. She threw her head back, flung her arms wide, and spun around, relishing, savoring the sight of the golden harvest moon in the star-sprinkled sky.

I looked up to see what so enthralled her and saw, for the first time in a long time, what she saw—hundreds of stars twinkling like diamonds against the blackness of the night.

Jaclyn ran across the grass in a joyous zigzag, face tilted upward, exclaiming, "Hello, star! Hello, moon! Hello, 'nother star!"

My heart melted. The picture of this perfect moment will be etched in my memory forever.

~~~~~

We try to force the perfect moments in our lives. We are sure that this year our family will achieve that wonderful Christmas that we see on all the TV shows. The day comes and, in spite of all our best efforts, in spite of all the hours spent shopping and cooking and cleaning and wrapping, the kids fight. They ask to exchange the jacket we thought was perfect. The dog vomits on the carpet. That uncle has too much to drink. Our husbands give us something with a cord.

But maybe the perfect moment really was there all along, hidden from view. Maybe it happened when you got up early to stuff the turkey and had the luxury of a quiet house, and your hands wrapped around a hot mug of coffee. And in the still of the morning, before the disappointment had begun, you looked up at the sky and said a silent prayer of thanks for the birth of the Christ child. One magic moment in a day of chaos; it is enough.

My friend Kay, braver than I am, also attempted a perfect family Christmas card photo the year she had two toddlers. The picture she sent out was hysterical. In it, one child was flailing with an open-mouthed scream. The other was slipping off the lap of her husband who lost his glasses in his attempt to hold on. The message was clear: our life is messy. Everyone's is. And this is why perfect moments are to be cherished.

The joy is in the experience, not the score.

One of the many cruelties inherent in living in an orphanage is the profound sameness of daily life. The environment is restricted, and the children are exposed to very little beyond the cement walls of the surrounding courtyard. After adopting Jaclyn, in an attempt to shake her morose attitude and because we, too, were anxious to escape the close quarters of the hotel room, we began exploring her hometown in China. Slowly, she began to shake her near-catatonic sadness at the total upheaval in her life as her curiosity got the better of her. Even years later, she could remember with great clarity all the things she saw for the first time on those forays. It was as if she had been plucked out and transplanted into a new world. She marveled at everything, exclaiming "WOW" over things as commonplace to us as french fries. Even months after her adoption, I was not sure that there was anyone alive who delighted in the world's little wonders as much as Jaclyn. It was fun to take her to new places and just watch her reaction.

The first autumn after we adopted Jaclyn, Rick's new boss offered him two seats next to his own for a University of Michigan football game. Rick wanted to take Jaclyn, sure that she would love his favorite activity. I thought he was nuts. I practically slipped into a coma after the first quarter; how in the world would he keep a four-year-old girl who knew nothing about football entertained?

And to take an unpredictable, rambunctious child to an event where your new boss was going to be? A major gamble even in the best of circumstances. However, I secretly relished the thought of a quiet Jaclyn-less afternoon, so I did not try to dissuade him.

Contrary to my prediction, Jaclyn was not at all bored at the game. In fact, she had a ball. She also entertained the U of M fans seated in their section. She shrieked so excitedly when she spotted a balloon on the loose that several rows of fans made valiant efforts, risking life and limb, to catch it so they could have the honor of presenting it to her.

She quickly dubbed Rick's new boss "Uncle Frank." Caught up in her enthusiasm, he gave her a personal tour of the stadium and bought her a small pizza.

When Jaclyn spotted a Michigan fan with a large beer belly wearing a blue plastic wolverine hat, she pointed. "Look, Daddy. That man has a skunk on his head. And he's going to have a baby!"

She squealed when she saw the marching band and danced to the music with a complete lack of self-consciousness. "When I hear the music, I feel the music!" she exclaimed. She screamed and cheered as loud as she wanted without any adults trying to quiet her. As a matter of fact, the adults were screaming too.

The stranger sitting beside Jaclyn shared peanuts with her. Jaclyn, who had never eaten peanuts, loved cracking open the shells to find the treat inside. Uncle Frank bought her a Michigan wallet. It was a fabulous day for her. And she never even knew the score.

When Jaclyn told me with unbridled enthusiasm about her afternoon, it made me think about when and how we lose the wonder in our lives. Someday Jaclyn will go to the stadium and be like the rest of us—focused on whether her team won or lost and oblivious to the joy of the experience itself. Children bring the wonder back into our lives. Until I saw Jaclyn's reaction, I had never stopped to realize how fun it really is to crack open a peanut shell. I couldn't even remember the last time I had really let myself feel the music and move to it. And the warmth of sunshine on your face on a fall afternoon when the chill of winter is just around the corner? Delicious.

When my girls were small, and I was always trying to hurry them along, just the route from our front door to the car would be filled with all kinds of neat things to look at . . . a dead bug, a muddy puddle, a swarm of ants crawling on a cast-off crumb. Things I had never noticed until I heard them squeal, "Look, Mommy!" And sometimes, not as often as I should have, I would stop hurrying and really look. Children teach us to slow down, to see what is around us. They teach us to be in the moment.

The true recipient of any gift is the giver.

Ten-year-old Jaclyn came to me while I was busy making the bed and moaned, "Mama, I just can't take it anymore. We need to get a baby in this house!"

Jaclyn had let me know, on numerous occasions, that her sister Christy, a soon-to-be-eight-year-old, did not fit the criteria of a baby.

"Jaclyn, I'm too old for another baby."

She looked at me sternly. "You didn't seem too old when you were jumping on the trampoline at Aunt Sandy's house last week."

"Well, I am too old," I insisted. "You'll just have to accept that."

Determined to have the last word she turned away and said over her shoulder, "I think you need to pray about it."

I shook my head at her persistence and finished straightening the comforter.

A few days later, as our family was getting ready to go to a party, Jaclyn said, "I've decided we need to get five babies from China."

"Five babies?" I exclaimed.

"Yes. Three boys and two girls."

"Where would they sleep?" I asked, amused by her obviously outlandish notion.

"We can put them all on one bed if we arrange them like this." She demonstrated with her hands how they could lie horizontally, as she remembered doing while in a medical facility in China.

"What about when they get too big for one bed?"

"Bunk beds." Jaclyn had obviously thought this through.

"What about your education?" I asked in an attempt at a reality check.

"Homeschooling," Jaclyn replied. "Just get me a tutor."

"I can't take care of all those children."

"Don't worry. I'll take care of them all by myself. You don't even need to help me." Jaclyn had an answer for everything. She had to have the last word.

I tried the oldest trick in parenting—diverting her with a new topic. I told her to finish getting dressed for Elizabeth's birthday party.

Elizabeth was turning four that day. My friend Sandy had adopted her from China a few months ago, and she rivaled Jaclyn in terms of strength of spirit and determination. And, like Jaclyn, Elizabeth seized life with both hands and a joyous heart.

For Elizabeth there was no walking—she had too much to experience, she had too much to see. She ran all day long, exploring
her world with a brilliant smile and a tiger-like tenacity.

Sandy ran behind her. I both pitied and envied Sandy. I knew
the exhaustion inherent in a child who always stretched the limits. But I also understood the joy of seeing the world through the
eyes of such a resilient soul.

Sandy had outdone herself to make sure this party was special
because she knew that in doing so she made the child feel special.
It was, after all, a celebration of life. As I surveyed the prepara-
tions she had made—the carefully strung streamers, the balloons,
the party hats, a pile of gifts, a bountiful buffet—I was reminded
of one of the truths that Jaclyn had told me long ago: "There's
no such thing as 'Happy Birthday' in China." For children in an
orphanage, one day is as mindlessly routine as another. Survival
was the goal; there were no resources for the celebration of the
uniqueness of any child.

Given this, how do you begin to celebrate the birth of a child
whose life had never been celebrated? A child whose birth date
is unknown because she was abandoned by her birth parents. A
child who had never known the surprise of a cake with her name
on it. Like me, all of the guests had come bearing gifts that added
to the sheer lunacy of the pile already assembled. How could we
make up for the deprivation she had known?

The room was filled with people I knew and loved. The three
couples there had all raised biological children, yet between us
we had made eight trips to China to adopt. All of us had been
changed from what we saw there. This common experience

bound us together, not only in our love for these kids but also in our understanding that what we had done in adopting them was so pitifully small in comparison to what needed to be done. Several of the adults had dedicated their careers—the manifestation of their love—to teaching children. I was honored to call them my friends.

Elizabeth's big brother, Steve, and his girlfriend, Lisa, who lived in Indiana, drove to Michigan for the party. Steve was thirty, and no one delighted in Elizabeth more than he did.

His other little sister from China, Katelyn, squealed, "Brother Steve!" at the first glimpse of him. He egged both girls on and laughed uproariously at their antics. He rough-housed with his little sisters, chased them, tickled them, and basically spoiled them. In watching them, I realized that this, too, was a gift that adoption had brought to our families—the chance to feel like kids again. The chance to have a celebration filled with laughter and the silliness and unbridled chaos that children bring to any occasion. And the chance to love a child again? The ultimate joy.

Elizabeth tore into her gifts with gusto, expressing exuberant delight with each item. When she exclaimed, "Wow!" as each present appeared, I couldn't stop tears from filling my eyes.

When the cake was brought out, everyone gathered around the table to sing "Happy Birthday" to Elizabeth. Her face radiated with such joy the candles seemed to lose their glow. It was a magic moment in a day filled with dreams that came true.

Before my family left, I hugged Sandy and thanked her for what she had given me—a day that I would never forget. I'd come thinking I was bearing the gift, but the truth was that I'd received a far greater gift—experiencing Elizabeth's happiness. Seeing the love reflected on the faces that watched her. The chance to celebrate with my favorite people. Priceless.

Driving home from the party, I thought about the two ways that there are to give a gift. The first is to feel slightly . . . resentful. "I brought such a nice gift to the family gift exchange, and *this* is what I got in return?" or "I'm invited to another shower? I hardly even know her." or "I hope he appreciates how much time and money I put into this!" Even if these sentiments aren't spoken aloud, they are thought more often than most people want to admit. My advice? Stay home; forget the gift. Don't ever give to another out of politeness, obligation, or with an expectation of thanks. There is really only one way to give a gift—with love.

Later that night as I put Jaclyn to bed, she began her prayers and, as always, had the last word: "Thank you, God, for giving Elizabeth a birthday party. But most of all, God, thank you for giving Elizabeth a *family*."

There is, after all, no greater gift than love.

The gift of perfect moments.

Too often, we shut out the joy of the moment, thinking that happiness lies somewhere in the future. *When I get married, I'll be happy. When I get that new house, I'll be happy. When my kids stop watching Barney 24/7, then I'll be happy. When my teenagers move out, I'll be happy.* When those milestones arrive, instead of being happy, we look ahead to the next target.

The time to be happy is now. The place to be happy is right where you are, no matter where that is.

We mistakenly think that happiness means being wrapped in euphoria that becomes our personal bubble wrap to protect us from the knocks in life. But the knocks still come. And happiness becomes an out-of-reach illusion.

I heard a woman say once that she had been happily married for fourteen years. Her friend looked at her in surprise and said, "But Rachel, you've been married for thirty years." Rachel replied, "I was happy for about six hours on Monday, seven minutes on Tuesday, and three hours on Wednesday. Based on that weekly average, I figure the total adds up to about fourteen years."

I think it's that way for all of us. We all want a fairy-tale marriage, a year where nothing bad happens, a happy life. There is no life filled with bliss; our happiness is the sum total of our joyful moments. And if we're always expecting fireworks, we'll risk missing those flickering, fleeting interludes of pure contentment.

In 2011, I took my teenage daughters on a mini-vacation that included a day at Universal Studios. We had an amazing time. The temperature was perfect—warm and sunny but not stifling hot. The lines were astonishingly short—we got to visit every attraction we wanted to see and rode some rides more than once. We had a great lunch of burgers and onion rings and milk shakes that we ate at an umbrella-covered table. For girls used to the Michigan tundra, it was a welcome winter respite. Near the end of the day, we got lemonade slushies and sat on a bench while a parade of Mardi Gras characters on stilts entertained us. We looked at each other and gushed, we actually gushed, about what a perfect day it had been.

Suddenly, as if on cue, a shower of white gook splattered down the front of my tunic and all over my purse. I looked up directly into the backside of a bird that seemed to have had the same gastrointestinal reaction to the greasy onion rings that I did.

I guess that's kind of an analogy for life. If you get too happy, something bad is bound to happen. But until the poop lands on you, savor the gift of perfect moments.

The Fourth Gift

Perspective

When I was in college, my roommates and I sometimes felt overburdened by what we thought was stress—mainly tests and homework and not having a date for a college formal dance. To relieve the tension, we sometimes challenged one another to a game of "Who Has the Worst Life?" The players all took turns reciting their complaints of the moment. The purpose of the game was to garner the most sympathy by being awarded the title of "Worst Life" for that day.

Little did we realize back then that many adults play a version of this game. They whine at work, grumble in the car pool, and complain at "girls' night out." They spew their tales of woe to anyone who'll listen.

In college I was the undisputed champion of the game. I won it once when I wasn't even playing. (I was in the hospital at the time.) I've had my share of knocks.

But I've never had cancer. I've never been robbed. I've never been homeless. I've never been in jail. I've never been hungry (with the exception of crazy, self-inflicted diets). In the bigger scheme of things, I'm pretty lucky.

There will always be people who have more than I do. And there will always be those who have less. That's probably true for you too.

If we spent as much time giving thanks for what we have instead of yearning for what we don't have, we'd be a lot happier. That view of the world is the gift of perspective.

What we see isn't always what it seems.

At Christmastime the year Jaclyn turned eight, she insisted on a private audience with Santa.

"What do you want to talk to Santa about?" I asked.

"Some of the kids in my class told me there's no such thing as Santa."

Jaclyn, who had been robbed of so much of her childhood, had loved fairy tales and stories of dreams that had come true more than any child I've ever seen. She had known too much heartache for one so young, and I wanted her to delight in childhood joys for as long as it was possible.

"So I thought of a way to tell for sure if there is a real Santa. I asked him for gum. If he brings it, I'll know there really is a Santa, because I know *you* would never give me gum." She smiled in delight at the intrigue.

Jaclyn loved gum, naming it as her favorite food. Being deprived of it for a year had been the most difficult part of having braces.

On Christmas morning, Jaclyn had a stocking full of gum. She clutched it to her, shut her eyes, and whispered, "I knew it!"

"What are you going to do with all that gum?" I asked. "You can't chew it with your braces on."

"I know," she said. "Maybe I can just lick it."

A few days after Christmas, we got the news that Jaclyn's braces were coming off a few months sooner than expected. For Jaclyn, everything fit together. God had known her braces were coming off and had filled Santa in on the news, just in time for the gum delivery.

Our final visit to the orthodontist was before school on a bitterly cold January morning, a day so frigid that the snowflakes stung our faces as we ran from the car into the office. As soon as the braces were off, after she had admired her new smile sufficiently in the mirror, I

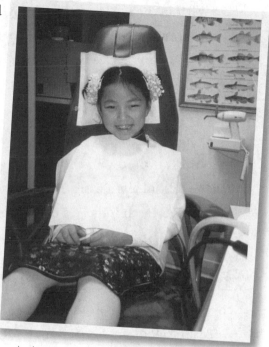

Jaclyn on the day her braces were removed

teased Jaclyn by asking: "When are you going to chew your first piece of gum?"

"I brought some in my backpack. It's out in the car." She giggled as she raced for the door.

Before going out into the frigid Michigan air, I knelt to zip Christy's winter coat. The zipper got stuck, and I had to struggle to free it. When I glanced out the glass door, I saw Jaclyn outside—without a hat, gloves, or boots, face turned skyward, pirouetting on the sidewalk as snow swirled around her ankles. I rushed to the door and shouted, "Jaclyn, it's freezing out here! Get in the car!" She lowered her eyes to meet my gaze, and it was obvious that my scolding did nothing to diminish her joy.

"What in the world are you doing?" I asked with thinly veiled exasperation when I reached her. She looked up at me, obviously surprised by my lack of understanding, and said, "I'm showing my smile to God!"

~~~~~

As you can imagine, I felt about two inches tall at that moment. I use this story now in the psychology classes that I teach to illustrate to students a basic truth: we see behavior, and we ascribe motive. Research indicates that we are almost always mistaken.

Just as I assumed that Jaclyn was doing something "wrong," so too do we judge others. They forgot to include us because they don't like us, because they intended to hurt us. We never conclude that they just forgot.

Assume good intent. Seek to understand first before you come to a conclusion. Think the best of others . . . and maybe God will show His smile to you.

Perspective is the difference between *disabled* and *differently abled.*

When my youngest daughter, Christy, began kindergarten, the first thing I noticed about her new teacher, Miss Kerri, was her welcoming smile. I also noticed her wheelchair and was secretly glad that Christy would have exposure at such a young age to someone who was physically challenged. It was important to me that my children understood and appreciated differences. I thought that, through knowing this teacher, she would have a wonderful learning opportunity.

As the months passed, I watched Miss Kerri with the children. It was evident by the joy with which she approached each day that she was born to be a teacher. She patiently allowed the children to play "train" with her. She'd let one student sit in her lap, one help push the wheelchair, and others line up behind her like train cars. She maneuvered throughout the school, smiling cheerfully while followed by a parade of little ones.

I kept waiting for Christy to ask about her teacher's physical challenges. I hoped to use her questions as a launching point to teach her about disabilities. Finally one day she told me, "Mama, Miss Kerri is different from the other teachers."

"Yes, she is," I said. "How have you noticed that she's different?"

Christy on Miss Kerri's lap— her favorite place

"She can always hear my voice!" For a little girl with a quiet voice, this was truly something special.

"Have you noticed any other ways that she's different?" I asked.

"Yes! She always has a lap to sit in!"

And to think I once believed that we teach our children. All I could see were Miss Kerri's limitations; it took a child's eyes to show me her special advantages.

And, through the lens of that perspective, I found myself understanding better the story of the Apostle Paul. My favorite parts of the Bible are his words; many of them were written when he was imprisoned. Paul was actually chained 24/7 to Roman guards. Many saw his circumstances and assumed that God had abandoned him. Paul saw an opportunity to accomplish two important tasks. He had a captive audience—literally—and so he began to share his message of hope and salvation with the guards who were chained to him. Many of those guards began to believe and eventually become the pillars of the Roman church. Second, the forced "down time" gave this busy preacher a chance to write down his thoughts in letters to his faraway friends—arguably the most powerful letters ever written.

Miss Kerri was trapped by her body; Paul was trapped by his circumstances. But neither was forsaken by God. In every trial there is an opportunity just waiting to be discovered.

Sometimes the best thing and the worst thing are the same thing.

When the girls were six, eight, and ten, they begged me to take them to the Friday evening Halloween party at their school. I looked forward to this event with the same enthusiasm I have for my dental check-ups. I am terrified of groups of sugar-rocketed little kids. Including my own.

I donated bags of assorted candy to school for the party. When Jaclyn discovered my candy bags contained gum, she warned me,

"We can't have that at school." I assured her it would be fine for the party, and the kids could take it home if it wasn't.

After months of agonizing over what costume to wear, ten-year-old Kate agreed to the idea of being Dorothy (which I actively promoted after finding the costume for fifty percent off).

Jaclyn, however, was very particular about what she would wear. None of the costumes we already had would do. So I took her to a resale store. I found a cowardly lion costume in Jaclyn's size and a scarecrow costume that would fit Christy perfectly. Visions of the Wizard of Oz trio danced in my head. Only one obstacle stood in my way—Jaclyn wanted to be a butterfly. She only wanted to be a butterfly. She could not be happy in life if she was not a butterfly. I begged. I cajoled. I pleaded. I surrendered. We got the butterfly costume. She hung it on her closet door and admired it for weeks.

On the afternoon of the party, the girls asked me every two minutes when they could put on their costumes. Finally, I relented. They described the elaborate hairdos they wanted to make their costumes just perfect. Jaclyn announced nonchalantly that she had decided she was not going to be a butterfly after all, but was going to wear a costume from the basement dress-up bin. I tried not to flinch as, working against type, she donned an angel costume.

Three girls piled in the car with heavy winter coats and candy buckets clutched tightly in their hands. The bitter wind howled furiously as we made the long trek from our parking spot several blocks away. The school was packed with so many families that it was hard to navigate the halls. Kate and Jaclyn ran for the trick-or-treat area, which was shrouded in mysterious dark lights while creepy sound effects reverberated from the walls. Christy took one look and burst into tears, so I let the older girls go alone if they promised to stay together.

Kate, Jaclyn and Christy dressed for the Halloween party

I took Christy to the cafeteria, figuring that if there was food, sooner or later Jaclyn would show up. When she did surface, she sampled every snack available, then flipped potato chips into her pop and fished them out to eat them.

She complained that her jaunt down the trick-or-treat hallway had not uncovered any gum. Nor did she spot any when she boldly examined other kids' candy bags.

"Mr. Beechum took it," she said. "I think that's what he does when he goes into his office and shuts the door. He chews gum!" Her eyes narrowed suspiciously. Yes, I was sure that was exactly what the principal did when no one was watching.

Christy, always one to find simple ways to entertain herself, now demanded a third trip to the bathroom. As soon as she was planted on the toilet, the fire alarm sounded. A mother rushed into the bathroom to tell me this was not a false alarm;

there was smoke in the hallway. I had no idea where the other girls were.

"Hurry, Christy, hurry."

"I can't. I have to go poo-poo!"

I stood there for what seemed an eternity, listening to the chaos outside the door as people scurried toward exits. I wavered between assuring myself that it was nothing and picturing us trapped in the bathroom while the school burned down.

Finally, Christy finished. She refused to skip the hand washing. By the time we rushed out into the hallway, the school had emptied. I wanted to search for my girls but was hustled outside by one of the staff. Clutching the coats they had left with me, I made my way out into the frigid, dark night and frantically called their names. The wind howled with such intensity that my voice didn't carry far. I fought a rising sense of panic as I pulled Christy along the icy grass. Sleet fell in sheets from the sky. Children screamed and cried all around me, but I couldn't find my girls anywhere.

Finally, the alarm stopped. Apparently the principal has been able to pull himself away from his surreptitious gum chewing long enough to investigate matters. The smoke had come from one of the special effects, and all was safe.

Christy and I went back inside with the crowd. I stood in the middle of the gym, still searching for the girls. Finally, Kate ran up to me, sobbing. "Mom, I couldn't find you anywhere. I was shivering so much that one of the moms zipped me into her coat. I was so scared!" She huddled against my body. "This party is awful!"

I put my arms around her. "I'm so sorry, honey. Should we all leave?"

"In a few minutes," Kate agreed. "The music is starting." She ran off to listen to the disc jockey blaring tunes.

The loud music and confusion reduced Christy to sniffles. I sat on a chair in the corner of the gym and held her. She insisted on keeping her jacket zipped and her hood up in case there was another fire drill. "Cover my eyes from the scary faces," she begged. She pointed out the costumes that frightened her while I shielded her eyes. I held my hands over her ears and gently rocked her while she softly moaned, "Can we go home?" over and over. She pulled her hood over her eyes to try to block out the whole party. I felt like doing the same thing.

When the DJ played Shania Twain's "I Feel Like a Woman," Christy jumped off my lap, ripped off her snow jacket, and flung it to the floor. "I love this song!" She raced out to the center of the dance floor and swung her tiny hips while belting out, "Whoa-ho-ho, I feel like a woman!" I swallowed my surprise and joined her. At the end of the song, she put her jacket back on and resumed her cowering. I continued to rock her.

A conga dance line formed as the song "Locomotion" rang out. Whenever any line forms, Jaclyn is right in the middle of it. Sure enough, I soon saw her. The second time the line passed, Jaclyn was nearly at the front. By the third go-round, she was leading the conga line.

After the dance ended, Jaclyn resumed her favorite activity— chasing the boys around the gym. She would fix her smile on any boy she recognized, begin to giggle, and then start to chase him around the gym.

"My wings are in my way," she said as she deposited part of her costume in my lap. Then she took off after her next hapless victim.

When I got worn down by Christy's incessant whining, I decided it was time to go. Christy clung to my leg in terror as I attempted to corral the other girls. I advanced slowly, pulling her along in a peg-legged gait.

I found Kate and told her it was time to leave. Before I could get her in her coat, she edged away. "I have to say goodbye to Tiffany." I caught up to her again. She wiggled away once more. "I didn't hug Lizzie goodbye yet!" And on and on it went.

I finally succeeded in cornering Jaclyn and told her it was time to go. "Just one more chip!" She ran off. I followed her as best I could, still dragging Christy along. Kate ran to the other side of the gym to hug another friend goodbye. They continued to slip away from me, elusive as eels, as I determinedly made my peg-legged romp around the gym trying to get them both within my grasp at the same time.

When we finally got home, I fumbled to unlock the door while holding Jaclyn's coat, her angel wings, three candy buckets, and Kate's Toto basket. I collapsed inside. My husband lifted his head from his peaceful snooze on the couch and said, "Did you stop to get milk?"

Amazingly, my head did not pop off from the steam coming out of my ears.

Jaclyn collapsed onto the stairway and wiped perspiration from her brow. "I need a drink!" My sentiments exactly. The evening was a disaster. But there was still one issue to resolve.

I felt enormous mommy-guilt for not finding Jaclyn during the fire drill. Her trust was still tenuous, and I was sure she had been even more rattled than Kate by being made to evacuate the school under such frightening circumstances. I sat next to her on the steps.

"I'm so sorry I couldn't find you during the fire drill, honey. Were you cold? Did you cry? Were you scared?"

She looked at me as if she had no idea what I was talking about. "That was so much fun! They never let us go out in the snow without our coats on. We never get to do cool stuff like that at school. I caught snowflakes on my tongue! Running around outside—that was the very *best* part."

To Kate, the fire alarm was terrifying and horrific; to Jaclyn, it was a chance to run unencumbered by a coat and taste the flakes falling from the sky. Perspective is the difference between horrible and wonderful.

Years ago I had to fire a woman from the bank where I worked. And even though she was doing a really crummy job, I dreaded the task. She came back a few years later to see me; I was sure she would deliver a tirade of bitterness. Instead she said, "In the beginning, I thought getting fired was the worst thing that could happen to me. Finally, I realized that I was doing poor work because I hated that job and wasn't at all suited to it. But I would have stayed there forever if you hadn't fired me. By doing that, you freed me to find the work I was meant to do. I did—and I want to thank you."

A setback or a new beginning? It all depends on your perspective.

There's always a silver lining.

One morning at breakfast, the girls were watching a PBS kids' show about a blind woman gardening with the help of her leader dog. Our local newspaper had done a series that week following several blind individuals through their day. After reading it, I realized how incredibly grateful I am for the gift of sight.

I saw this as an opportunity to share with the girls how grateful we should be for our vision. I spoke passionately about all the things I loved to see. I explained how challenging it would be to have to rely on a leader dog. I then asked them if they would help me if I ever became blind.

My sweet Kate chimed in, "Of course, Mom. We'd help you do everything if you were blind."

Pragmatic Jaclyn had a different take on things: "At least then we could get a dog!"

I chuckled at the time, but there is often a hidden blessing in even the most trying situation. It reminded me of the story of my close friend Tammy. Her teenaged son, Ian, was involved in a foolish prank that went horribly wrong; he ended up in jail. It was any mother's worst nightmare, and Tammy was filled with fear. In looking back on that time, she told me, "It was, without a doubt, the most horrible thing that ever happened to my family. I can remember crying out to God in that court room, begging him not to forsake my son. I realize now it was the first time I ever felt close to God. And that was a gift that has never left me. The year before Ian's arrest, my husband and I had separated. We were quickly heading for divorce. But we clung to each other during that trying time. That tragedy helped us find our way back to each other; it saved my family."

The best thing and the worst thing often spring from the same circumstances. The secret is staring boldly into the darkness and finding the glimmer of light.

Sometimes the difference between a bad day and a good day is a hug.

Moms are not allowed to be sick. Ever. Not even the briefest of naps is permitted.

On one such day, after I explained to the girls that they were not to wake me for anything but an emergency, and that "emergency" meant that someone was bloody or something was on fire, I was still poked by tiny fingers for emergencies like "I found a dime under the couch."

Every ten minutes, I heard "Are you still sick?" There is clearly a statute of limitations on the amount of time a mom can be out of commission.

But when the kids have the slightest sniffle, the world immediately comes to a standstill.

A case in point was Christy's bladder infection when she was four years old. This emergency trip to the doctor occurred on a day when my other two daughters had half-days at summer camp. In my rush to pick up the older girls for the appointment, I forget to bring my bag of amusements. Unarmed, all of us landed at the pediatrician's office on what was clearly a very busy afternoon.

I knew a urine sample would be part of the ordeal, and being the quick-thinking mother I am, I asked for a specimen cup immediately upon arrival. Filled with the soda I'd bought on the way, Christy was ready to go. I took her to the bathroom and explained the drill as she eyed the specimen cup suspiciously. I placed her on the toilet and bravely held the cup underneath her. The older girls watched the proceedings with intense interest.

"I'm ready to go now, Mama," Christy said.

"Go ahead." I poised like an outfielder ready to catch a fly ball.

"I can't go with your hand in the toilet!"

I explained the process again, justifying my position. Finally, sobbing and mortified, she peed. I moved my hand all around, trying to catch a few drops. My fingers dripping with urine, I pulled out the specimen cup.

"Ew, yuck!" Jaclyn shrieked. "That's disgusting!"

As soon as I set it down on the floor, Christy accidently kicked over the specimen cup. I dove for it, making a save that would impress any major league player. As I looked at the pitifully few drops of urine clinging to the sides, I nearly cried.

"What's the doctor going to do with that?" Jaclyn asked.

"She's going to look at it . . . " I mumbled while scrubbing my hands.

"She's going to *lick* it?" Jaclyn shrieked in horror.

"No, I said *look*."

"You said *lick*," Jaclyn insisted.

I went to the nurses' station to see if anyone would take the specimen cup before it was knocked over again, but they insisted that I keep it. While I was busy talking to the nurse, all three girls were busy too—busy jumping on the waiting room ottomans and shrieking with laughter. I turned around, incredulous at the sight of the same child—who had been sobbing so hysterically that I had begged for an immediate doctor's appointment—now jumping with glee. Christy's name was called three times before I heard it over the din.

We proceeded to a tiny cubicle. The nurse approached Christy with the blood pressure cuff, and I assured her it would just feel like her arm was getting a hug.

"Christy," Jaclyn said, her eyes wide, "it feels like a big snake wrapped around your arm and squeezing you tight!"

Christy whimpered. But this was only the warm-up.

Because of the urgent nature of our visit, we got a new doctor who was intent upon knowing Christy's full medical history. Jaclyn was equally intent upon knowing the doctor's history.

"Who are you? How old are you? Where did Dr. Cheng go? Why don't you have any crayons in here? What's in that drawer? Can I get a sticker? Do you have any suckers?" Jaclyn barely paused between questions.

As the doctor filled out her coding sheet, Jaclyn asked, "What's that? Why are you coloring in all those dots? Can I color too?"

The doctor tried to distract her by posing her own question. "How many people are in your family?"

Before I could open my mouth, Jaclyn piped up: "Sixteen, including my godparents, my aunt and uncle, my cousins . . . " She droned on with way more family history than anyone would care to hear.

Without my bag of tricks, I was impotent to silence Jaclyn.

While I attempted to talk to the doctor, the girls repeatedly popped open the garbage can by stepping on the foot pedal, wrote their names on the tissue box, scooted around on the doctor's wheeled stool, looked into every drawer, and launched into a tap-dance routine on the linoleum. The doctor looked at me suspiciously while I tried to convince her that one of them was actually sick.

Finally, it was time for the examination.

"Why you looking in there?" Jaclyn asked as the doctor checked Christy's ears. "What you looking for?"

"Does it hurt all the time or just when you go pee-pee?" the doctor asked Christy.

"Just when I go pee-pee."

"Oh! She said pee-pee!" Jaclyn tattled.

"It's okay to say that to the doctor," I whispered.

"Well, it's still not a *nice* word!" Jaclyn scolded the doctor.

The doctor stepped out for a moment. The girls continued to bounce off the walls.

"I'm going to draw some blood," she said when she returned.

"You can't draw anything in here," Jaclyn said with annoyance, "because there aren't any crayons."

I stifled a nervous chuckle. The doctor's face turned red.

"These tests will only take about ten minutes," she assured me. She clearly had no idea how long ten minutes could be to someone trapped in an eight-foot-square cubicle with no distractions and three small children.

The nurse asked me to hold Christy while she took six vials of blood.

Jaclyn's eyes widened in horror. "Look at all the blood! Ew, gross!" She peered suspiciously at the nurse. "What are you going to do with all that blood?"

I held Christy close and tried to distract her by pointing out the piggies on the wallpaper. But I was no match for Jaclyn.

"Does that big needle hurt, Christy? How much? Does it hurt really bad? Does it hurt really, really bad?"

When we were finally allowed to leave, I looked at the clock. Amazingly, only ninety minutes had passed. I was sure we'd been in that cubicle for at least three days.

As we stood in the interminable line at the drugstore waiting for the prescription, Christy asked, "Mama, what was your favorite part of going to the doctor's?"

"Leaving," I answered without hesitation.

"Oh," she said with a crestfallen expression. "My favorite part was the holding. I loved it when you held me."

At bedtime I thought about her innocent words and the comfort that comes from having someone that you love to hold onto. Putting her to bed had always been my favorite moment of the day. She went to bed easily, but I have to confess that I prolonged those final moments of the day just so I could hold the snuggly warmth of her tiny body against mine. I would crawl into her bed and put my arms around her and listen to the gentle whisper of her sleepy breaths. My job was stressful and thankless. My marriage was slowly unraveling. I was totally exhausted from doing the tap dance required of one who is balancing the roles of wife, mother, and executive. But those moments when I held her, those magic moments when we held onto each other, they saved me. And gave me the strength to make it through another day.

It's all relative.

"I know God made everybody but Himself," five-year-old Jaclyn told me after Sunday school. "But where did the first baby come from?"

I knew the answer to this one. "First, God made Adam and Eve, and they had the first baby."

"Is Eve the boy and Adam the girl?"

"The other way around. Then they had more babies, and those babies had babies, and pretty soon there were lots of people."

Jaclyn thought about this and then said, "If all the people came from the same mommies and daddies, then we're all family, right?"

I'd used the terms "the family of man" and "all God's children" before but had never thought of their literal meaning.

Jaclyn threw her arms open and said, "The whole world is just one big family."

I paused for a moment, reflecting on that simple truth. I've witnessed some pretty nasty battles within families. What amazed me most weren't the stupid things that blew up into major altercations, the harsh words that were said to those who are loved most, or the sheer lunacy of the drama. What amazed me most is the way that most family members find a way back to each other. We try because, in the end, we are bound together. We try even when it is really hard.

On the other hand, we are often quick to write off those who have offended us in other arenas of our lives. We nod curtly to the neighbor who hurt our feelings, we avoid the colleague who criticized our project; it's easier to shut them out than to mend fences.

But what if we embraced Jaclyn's truth—that we are all family? Somewhere, somehow, in some distant past, we have shared ancestry. What divides us is smaller than what should unite us: we all love our kids. We all want to leave this earth better than we found it. We all respect kindness. In every corner of the world, we know what a smile signifies. Our tears are interchangeably salty. Laughter sounds the same. And maybe we'd try harder too, to find a way to cooperate, to mend riffs, to accept without judgment, if we thought of ourselves as sisters and brothers—flawed and imperfect and challenging and occasionally down-right annoying, but worth the effort. Just like family.

Beauty is measured by the sum of our hearts.

As the girls entered adolescence, I realized I would face numerous challenges. But one of the most annoying was their endless scrutiny in the mirror. In our house we all shared one bathroom. Getting ready in the morning nearly always resulted in tears as these harsh critics scrutinized their imperfections.

"I look fat in these pants."

"My hair is always greasy."

"Everyone will laugh at my huge zit!"

"Why are my eyes so small?"

These self-inflicted criticisms were the veneer over the secret worries of every teenage girl—What if others judge me by my appearance? What if I'm not accepted? And the biggie: What if I'm not pretty enough to ever be loved?

In high school, Kate was beautiful and popular. She became the varsity pom-pom champion. She had friends galore and was rarely without a love interest. But all that did nothing to reassure her when she looked in the mirror. She hated having brown eyes; blue eyes were better. Why did she have to get the Champnella hips? And her thumbs were clearly stubby.

When I looked at her, I couldn't see past the kindness in her heart. Kate had rushed upstairs to clear out dresser drawers for her new sister when she heard us talk of adoption. A year later, she willingly gave up her bedroom. She took on the bullies who tormented Jaclyn. She included Jaclyn with her older friends. She brought home french fries for Jaclyn when she went on a date. She climbed into Christy's crib to comfort her when she was a baby and never let her be sad or frightened.

My proudest moment came when I picked her up after her senior-year pom-team tryouts. The names of those who made the squad were displayed prominently on poster boards at the school entrance. The varsity girls whose names were on the list shrieked with glee and took turns hugging each other. Kate sat at the curb with her arms around two girls who didn't make it. While the girls sobbed, Kate hugged them and offered words of comfort.

Jaclyn was also gorgeous, and she had a killer smile. She was an accomplished athlete and a hard-working student, and she could put together an outfit that rivaled those in fashion magazines. But all that did nothing to reassure her when she looked in the mirror. Her toned athletic figure disappointed her. Her eyelashes weren't long enough. And her feet were much too wide.

When I looked at her, I couldn't see past the compassion in her heart. At seven years old, she had traveled the country with me, signing thousands of books telling her story with the selfless hope that by putting her story out there, other children would be adopted. She told anyone who would listen about all the kids in China still awaiting families. When she was four years old, she rushed to pick up crying babies in the orphanage and held them, mimicking the care of a mother even though she'd never known a mother's care herself. She holds the power of love to change lives.

And then there was Christy. A talented musician, a gifted student, and a loyal friend. But she saw nothing special when she studied her reflection in the mirror and expressed puzzlement and doubt when I told her otherwise.

When I looked at her, I couldn't see past the sweetness in her heart. She let me know, every day, how much she loved me. She thanked me for everything, taking nothing for granted. What humbled me most was how she thanked God for me.

When these beautiful, amazing young women looked at themselves, all they saw were the flaws. When I looked at them, all I saw was their hearts.

I sometimes think that's the way it is between us and God. We see our failings; He sees our hearts. As the old saying goes, beauty is in the eye of the beholder. And it's measured not by the sum of our parts, but by the sum of our hearts.

Too soon it's too late.

When I heard the words, I could not comprehend them. I got the phone call on a day when I sat at home feeling sorry for myself. I had a miserable cold and commitments that couldn't be cancelled. Poor me! I couldn't be sick; too many people needed me.

Then I heard from another adoptive mom that a beautiful little girl named Lynn Mei had died that day of a febrile seizure. She was not yet three years old. The words took my breath away and helped me put my puny woes into perspective.

My faith teaches that there is a reason for all things even though we can't always understand that reason. Our time on this earth is as if we are "looking through a glass darkly" (1 Corinthians 13:12), but one day we will understand all things. I've always believed that when that day came there would be no need for explanations.

But I want an explanation for this.

I met Lynn Mei's parents when I worked as an adoption social worker. Julie desperately wanted to be a mom. And she knew with absolute certainty that a daughter awaited her in China. Julie completed the voluminous paperwork in record time. As she endured the long wait for a referral, she prayed daily for her daughter. She and her husband, Mark, couldn't wait to begin this new chapter in their life.

No one knew how short that chapter would be.

Upon entering the funeral home, I saw Julie and tried to imagine what it would be like to bear a loss of this magnitude. It was a horror beyond comprehension.

Our society has descriptors for those who survive loss. If you lose your spouse, you're called a widow or a widower. Without my husband's love, I would be as unsteady as a newborn colt. But my mind understands that there is a 50/50 possibility that I will someday walk on this earth without him.

If you lose your parents, you're called an orphan. Although I can hardly envision what my life would be without my mother, my biggest fan, my first source of comfort and support, I know that if events unfold in a natural sequence, someday I will be parentless.

But to lose a child? Our society has no word to describe a survivor of this tragedy—perhaps because there are no intact survivors of such a loss. How do you continue to move forward, much less eat, sleep, love, and live? When you put your own heart into the ground, do you also bury all your hopes and dreams for the future? Or do you find yourself fearless when the worst thing a mother can face has already happened? Do you become brittle and break as you shut out the goodness in life? Does the pain ever dull? Is there any day when this loss is not the first thought in your mind upon waking and the final thing you carry with you into your fitful dreams?

I was afraid to speak to Julie because I knew her grief could be mine but for the grace of God. I could not stand there, as she did, with grace and fortitude, answering questions and giving hugs and introducing people and reaching out, in spite of the enormous gash in my heart. I could not stand there, period.

Mark was a tall man, but when I saw him there, he seemed shrunken. It was as if having the joy sucked out of him somehow made him physically smaller. I will never forget the look of pain in his eyes. I hope I never see that kind of pain again.

I did not know their daughter, Lynn Mei, in life. Julie and Mark were no longer my clients when her adoption became final, and the endless details of life had kept us apart. So I sat near the back of the chapel and watched on a TV screen the images of the beautiful child and her world. I could not stop the choking sobs that racked me. I didn't even try.

I saw a picture of her poised in front of a birthday cake, hands outstretched even before it was out of the box, as if she couldn't wait to sneak a lick of frosting with her finger. And I thought of all the times I had told my children not to lick their fingers.

I saw a picture of her with her mouth open wide in a laugh, a squeal, a shout. And I thought of all the times I had told my children to be quiet.

I saw a picture of her riding on her father's back. And I thought of all the times I begged my kids to get down because my arms ached.

I saw a picture of three pairs of shoes sitting by the front door. A large pair of men's white sneakers next to a medium-sized pair of women's sneakers next to a tiny pair of children's sneakers. And I thought of all the times I had yelled at my kids to pick up their shoes as I tripped over them in the foyer.

I saw the pictures of the three of them doing simple, every-day things—walking down the sidewalk, sitting together in the grass, playing in the pool. And I thought of all the nights I had worked late and missed those moments, thinking I could make them up tomorrow.

What if tomorrow never comes?

Life at its most abundant is in the simple moments of joy that sneak up on us when we're not too busy doing. And the measure of our time here is how many of those moments we savor.

In remembrance of Lynn Mei, I want to embrace the finger-licking, boisterous, exhausting, messy moments of childhood. And give my kids an extra hug every night.

Thanks, Lynn Mei, for the gift of perspective.

The Fifth Gift

Parenting

On one Mother's Day, my older sister, Willow, had a family dinner at her home to honor our mom. Before the meal began, she suggested we all share stories about moms as a way of honoring this special day.

Willow started the ball rolling by remembering a time when she sprang on Mom at ten p.m. that she needed forty oranges cut into fancy designs and stuffed with fruit for an ethnic food presentation in Spanish class the next day. When she woke in the morning, she found that Mom had labored long into the night so Willow had her assignment. Yes, Mom was definitely a hero.

Our mother beamed, expectantly waiting for the next wonderful memory to be shared.

Before I could sort through my thoughts and select the best story, my oldest daughter, Kate, piped up. "I have a good story about my mom."

I smiled modestly in anticipation.

"Last year at Aunt Willow's Christmas party, she had these really cute miniature Coke bottles in the fridge. I asked my mom if she would take one home for me because I really liked them. But she said, 'I can't steal something from my sister's house.' Then when we got home, she slipped one out of her purse! We named it Elmer, and it's still in the back of our fridge."

My sister looked at me in shock. "You stole something from my house? Gee, I hope you don't sneak out with the candlestick holders tonight! Honestly, you didn't have to take it. If you'd just asked, I would have given it to you."

Beet red, I stammered to explain as my entire family stared at me.

Jaclyn saved me by saying that she had a story about me to share. I could hardly wait.

"I was at the swim club with my friends, and Mom was wearing this really gross tan-colored bathing suit. One of my friends said, 'Look at that lady! She doesn't look like she has a bathing suit on!' I was glad no one knew it was *my* mom! I just acted like I was grossed out too. Which I was."

It's nice to know that my children will remember me as a naked thief.

I'd be the first to admit that I will never win Mother of the Year. I am not particularly gifted as a parent. But parenting has been the greatest gift in my life.

This gift took me by surprise since I had spent so much time and energy on *not* becoming a parent. A product of the 1970s, the first generation of women to actually have choices, I came of age on the cusp of the clamoring for equal rights for all women. I put off becoming a mom until my biological clock was ticking so loud it was undeniable. Even then, I figured I would only have one child so I could get right back to my career.

When I heard women say how difficult it was to be a working mom, I'd thought the hard part was the logistics—like how to get the kids dropped off at day care and still get to work on time. When I became a mom myself, I quickly realized that the hard part was that you never, ever wanted to have your children out of your sight. You can't imagine anyone else looking at their sweet smiles all day or wiping their tears. What if they stumbled and fell and got hurt and you weren't there to fix it for them?

I called my mother to confront her. Why had she not told me *this* was what I was missing? Why hadn't she pushed me to become a mother sooner? She sighed deeply and said, "There isn't a way to explain it to anyone else. You have to feel it for yourself." Then she added, "Actually, I think it's a great blessing that people who aren't parents don't know what it feels like. Because if they really knew what they were missing, they wouldn't be able to bear it."

This is not to say that parenting is all bliss. Years ago my mother confessed that my divorce was the worst thing that had ever happened to her. At the time I was miffed because, honestly, it happened to *me*. It wasn't about her. But years later, when I literally fell to my knees from the wrenching pain in my heart when my own daughter was being bullied, I understood. When your children hurt, you are wounded beyond words. The love you feel for a child is multiplied exponentially beyond any other love. So is the pain.

Parenting is tough. It's demanding. Tiring. Exciting. Rewarding. Parenting is happiness beyond words. It is our love manifested. It is our one chance to reach beyond ourselves and shape the future. Parenting is, without a doubt, one of the greatest gifts of life.

> Our children are never really our own;
> they are simply on loan from God.

On a warm spring day early in May, I heard the words I'd dreaded for a long time. I knew it would happen. I knew I would not escape without hearing it said out loud. But I thought I had time to come up with the right response. Time to brace myself for the pain. I didn't think that time was now.

I had picked up five-year-old Jaclyn at school, and when she took her seat in the back, where she could talk without making eye contact, she said simply, "Nate says you're not my *real mama.*"

The fist in my gut had landed.

Nate was Jaclyn's intended future husband. She had claimed him early on, reasoning that the middle boy in a family of three brothers was a perfect match for her, the middle sister. His word carried a lot of meaning for her.

"Of course I'm your real mom, Jaclyn, you know that," I responded with more fierceness than I intended.

My head spun with all the connotations of not being "real." Was my longing for this child of my heart not real? Was my desire to make her mine not real? What about my fear of what would happen to my very soul if she did not become mine? Or the love that brought me halfway around the world to claim her? Was my joy and pride in being her mother not real?

My emotions triggered the one thought I always pushed away to the farthest corner of my mind: who was Jaclyn's real mom? The one who left her, or the one who brought her home? The one who gave birth to her and didn't keep her, or the one who didn't give her life but wanted to keep her always? I was filled with an overwhelming sense of unfairness at how giving birth somehow elevated a woman to the place of "realness," while my lifelong efforts seemed to give me the second-place title.

I pushed aside my own feelings to give Jaclyn the assurance she was seeking that I would always be her mother. And that "real" had nothing to do with biology and everything to do with love.

Before I could speak, she said, "I missed you the whole time I lived in China."

My heart melted. I was touched by her sureness that the mom who was meant for her would eventually come. How could she have been so certain when there was not one hopeful sign, when she had waited so long?

Then she added her own explanation. "My China mama just borrowed me."

As much as I wanted to believe that she belonged to me, I knew she was just on loan to me too. How grateful I felt that God had entrusted me with His treasure, for whatever years remained until she was grown and ready to make her own way in the world.

But guilt nagged me as I thought about how quickly I had claimed this crown. To assert that I was the only real mom trivialized another woman's contribution. Was I saying that her birth mother's morning sickness, her swollen ankles, her joy or sorrow at the news of the pregnancy were not real? Or the flickers of life she felt when she carried Jaclyn? Or her pain in labor and delivery, most likely without any medical comforts or relief? Or her care and love and attention to her baby? Or her angst in making her choice? Or the sorrow she carried in her heart, probably to this day?

I could only imagine the cavernous hole in my heart that could never be filled if I lost Jaclyn, and she had been my child for less than one year. Her birth mother knew her for much longer. How huge must the gash in her soul be? Isn't she, too, entitled to be *real?*

Christy at a year old – what a smile!

And what about all the others who cared for her, provided for her, and loved her before I did? Her Chinese grandmother picked Jaclyn up on her bicycle each morning, carried her to her home in a basket, and lovingly washed, dressed, and cared for her while her mother worked. And what about the woman who found Jaclyn when she was abandoned, cleaned her up, got her urgently needed medical care, then brought her to the police station? What about the nannies at the orphanage? And the two women who tried to adopt her before I did? I knew they all still loved her. Weren't they real too?

To be an adoptive parent means that we always have to share the credit. Whether our children are ours by birth or adoption, we can't claim them as solely our own. They are part of something bigger—a circle of love that extends well beyond our households into the far corners of this world.

The truth was I thought of my adopted girls' moms often. The complexity of those feelings were hard to sort out. I couldn't begin to imagine what the loss of their daughters was like for them.

When Christy was baptized, I wrote a letter filled with love and thanks to her unknown birth mom, and we ceremoniously released it, tied to a bright red balloon, into the sky. But on her third birthday, I found that I still had much to share with this unknown woman. So I sat down a second time to empty my heart. Knowing the letter would never reach its intended recipient, I wrote:

Dear Christy's Birth Mom,

Today I celebrate our daughter's third birthday. She has been my daughter for two and a half years and, somehow, for a lifetime too. I can hardly remember a time when I didn't know her, when I did not have the love of this child in my life.

When I first saw her picture, I knew her. I knew her with such intensity that it was agony to not be able to hold her right then. My bags had been packed for the adoption trip to China for six weeks. I have never anticipated anything with as much pure joy as I did my first meeting with her.

The night I adopted her, I woke in sobs, thinking of you. And shuddering, trembling, at the realization of the magnitude of your loss.

It's strange that I should think of you now as my dear friend. Before I adopted her, I thought of you as my rival. I would never have considered a domestic adoption because of my fear of having to know a birth mother. I somehow thought we would be competitors for the same prize. How foolish of me to think as if she only had a finite amount of love and not enough for both of us to share.

For if there ever was a child with enough love to go around, it is this one. When I asked her orphanage nanny to describe her personality, she said, "This baby likes to love." And it's true. She hugged me at our first meeting and has not stopped nuzzling me since. Sometimes she comes to me, and when I ask her what she wants, she says simply, "I want you." She is the most loving little soul I have ever known. How sorry I am that you cannot feel her sweet embrace, her soft caresses, and her gentle kisses.

Sometimes my husband and I fight over her. Neither of us can bear to ever leave her behind. So maybe it is best you left her when you did. Because if you had begun to know her, you would never have been able to do what you needed to do.

New life is created by acts of love; her life is no exception. Your loving act, your courage in bringing her to a safe place, is what created her new life.

I cannot imagine what this sacrifice did to your soul. In my mind's eye I have seen you surrender her so many times. I can picture you, in the cover of darkness, laying down your precious burden and bestowing a final kiss on her sweet cheek. How did you find the courage to walk away?

I too have felt life stir inside me. I know the love a mother has for her child before it is born. It would be easier for me to rip my own heart out than to have to do what you did. I would die. Is that how it was for you? Are you a person who appears living, but is truly dead inside?

All I can offer in comfort is that shortly after your surrender, something in me came alive. Maybe this is how it was destined to be between us—a perpetual seesaw as the depths of your sorrow match the heights of my joy. I offer as consolation that if her radiant smile is any indication of the joy in her soul, she is very happy in her new life.

I guess I don't have to tell you that she is beautiful; that must have been evident from the moment she drew her first breath. I believe that this beauty is what saved her life; her orphanage has only ever placed five children for adoption. I can't help but think that this is what distinguished her from the rest and made her one of those chosen for adoption.

I take special pleasure in her beauty in a way I could not if she had my genetic material in her. And I am not ashamed to admit the truth. No child born of my body could have the radiant, rare-orchid beauty of her face, the subtle grace of her movements, the angel fingers and delicate feet that she possesses.

She is beautiful on the inside too. She is a gentle soul. She is shy with strangers, speaking in a sweet whisper that makes them bend close to hear her thoughts.

When I returned to Fogang City, the place of her birth, I found myself searching the faces of the women in the town. I felt certain I would be able to recognize you if I saw you, just as I had recognized her as my daughter when I first saw her picture. It seemed impossible to imagine that we could share so much and still be strangers to each other.

She listens to me pray for you at night when I put her to bed. Now, she has no comprehension of who you are and your significance to her. She does not know that without you, she would not exist. That is why I pray for you. I have no other way to thank you for what you gave her: life. And what you gave me: the joy of my life. I wonder if I will feel differently when she understands the bitter pain of the absence of you. Will I feel less loving toward you? Will I be less satisfied with all the love she so freely gives if she saves a part of it for you?

And here's another paradox of adoption. Even though I think of you so often, I also forget that she is not a child of my body. We went to

Disney World recently, and while she was playing in a crowded area, under my watchful eye, another parent approached me. He pointed to her and said, with more than a little concern, "I've been here a long time, and I haven't seen her parents here anywhere!" At first I felt indignant, thinking the remark was a commentary about my attentiveness. It took a few moments for me to realize that my blonde hair and fair skin had led him to conclude that we could not possibly be mother and daughter. I forget sometimes that the bond that is so strong between us can be invisible to strangers.

Because she is mine in a way that is so powerful and encompassing, I can hardly speak of my love for fear I will be at a loss for words big enough to describe it. How many hours have I spent cradling her precious body, cherishing the sweet smell and the tender touch of her? I laugh when I think of all my fears about being able to love an adopted child the same as my biological child. How foolish that seems now!

Did I tell you she has sisters? When she first met her older sister, Kate, she held on to her finger tightly, evidencing none of the fear she had of other children. She somehow knew that Kate was a gentle soul. And Jaclyn? They wrestle like little puppies, rolling over each other in a pile of giggles. In China, because of the one-child-per-family policy, she would never have known the joy of siblings; this is one gift she has been given. And if you could see her holding hands with her two big sisters, the comfort she gets from their loving care, the pride they have in showing her off, you would know, as I do, that she is blessed to have sisters like these.

I do not know yet if she possesses any special talents or gifts beyond this one: she knows how to love. She loves with her whole being. And when I see all the people in this world who are stingy with their love, I think that this is, perhaps, the greatest gift of all.

I will understand if, one day, the laws change in China and she wants to find you. A part of me searches for you too and wants to know who you are. When I look at her, I sometimes wonder if her beautiful eyes are yours. The smile that brings tears to my eyes; was it your gift? As she reveals herself more to me over the years, I sense I will know you more. And so I wish for these things: a way to tell you she is safe and loved. A glimpse of your face. A moment to put my arms around you in a hug filled with love and compassion. A chance to dry your tears. A way to convey my deepest gratitude.

I promise you this: I will try to prove worthy of our daughter. I will do my best to convey to her your love, your strength, and your pain. I will not let her forget you.

Thank you for trusting me to teach the miraculous, irrepressible child that you grew under your heart all the lessons of living. Thank you for letting her grow each day in my heart.

Christy's other mom,
Cindy

If you want to make lasting change in this world, choose to love a child.

Almost from the start, Jaclyn let me know that my attempts at mothering were simply that—attempts. When I adopted her at the age of four, she came to me having lost one important innocence: the trust that any adult could be counted on to do the right thing, to care for her, to meet all her needs so she could become a carefree, dependent, and forgetful little girl, which is what a child should be. It was as if, from the beginning, she saw all my woeful inadequacies and determined to make the best of it anyway. After all, she had cared for herself—and two others—as a four-year-old in the orphanage. She simply continued in that same pattern once we brought her home.

Watching her manage not only her young life but also those of the others in our household became for me a source of both amusement and wrenching grief. There was simply no way to wave a magic wand and make her a child again. She had seen too much suffering, she had known too much sorrow, she had endured too much disappointment.

Early on, Jaclyn made little shots at the job I was doing parenting her younger sister, Christy. Jaclyn liked to point out to me that *her* baby (her beloved orphanage charge) did not wear diapers. Her commentary was usually accompanied by a withering glance at her two-year-old sister, who had no success in potty training. Because they shared a room, Jaclyn determined to keep Christy in line—there would be no slackers on her watch. Jaclyn could nag like no other. As the years passed, Christy was needled mercilessly about clothes thrown on the floor and toys that were not put away.

When Jaclyn was nine and Christy was seven, I noticed that Jaclyn had posted a list of rules on the door of their shared bedroom—for Christy's benefit. The list read:

1. Throw apple core in kitchen garbage when you are done.
2. Throw banana peels and other food garbage in the kitchen garbage.

3. If you have plates, bowls, and cups that have food on them, put them on the kitchen counter. Or you will not be able to eat up here.

THINK BEFORE DOING IT!!!

P.S. You have only 5 chances.

The number 5 in the P.S. had been crossed out and replaced with the number 4. Apparently, one of Christy's chances had already been burned.

Christy confessed to me that her secret dream in life was to have her own room. I wonder why.

Jaclyn knows how to solve problems. Christy did not like to get out of bed in the mornings, and we had all exhausted ourselves devising strategies to prod her along. But Jaclyn figured this one out. One morning she approached Christy's bed holding a plate of recently microwaved french fries. She waved them over Christy's sleepy nose with this promise: "If you get out of bed, I'll give you a french fry." It worked like magic.

A few days later, Christy said she had something to show me. It was a long piece of heavy yarn tied to her backpack. "Do you know what this is?" she asked me.

I shook my head.

"It's a leash," she replied indignantly. "Jaclyn pulls me by it if I don't walk fast enough on the way home from the bus stop!"

I stifled my giggles while sternly admonishing Jaclyn that she was *not* to pull her sister with a leash.

One Friday night, Jaclyn had two social events back-to-back—an ice cream party at school and a church sleepover at a local community center. When I arrived home to do the ferrying back and forth,

The "Princess Party" the girls threw for mom

Jaclyn greeted me at the door. "You're late! I have already missed eight minutes of fun."

I scrambled to make the first event, then drove across town like a maniac, through heavy traffic and pouring rain, to pick up her friend, bring her back, and deposit the girls at the sleepover. Unfortunately, when we arrived, there were almost two hundred kids waiting in line to register. This did not meet the approval of Miss Jaclyn. She narrowed her eyes at me and muttered loudly, "I knew we should have gotten here an hour early. I've missed twelve minutes of fun!" This mantra continued throughout the interminable wait in line. "Now they're eating doughnuts. I want to eat doughnuts!" Followed by "Now I've missed eighteen minutes of fun!" There were too many witnesses to choke her into silence, so I endured her unrelenting fuming. After all, disappointing Jaclyn just seemed to go with the territory.

A few weeks later, it was my birthday. The girls made a scavenger hunt for me, with the final clue leading to a party they had planned in their bedroom, which they had filled with balloons and streamers and lovingly drawn art. They seated me in a chair decorated as a throne and presented me with homemade cards.

Jaclyn presented her card last. Like the child herself, it was filled with words that brought both joy and anguish. The card began, "Dear Mom. You are the best. You are beautiful and nice. You are the world's greatest mom. I love you." I smiled until I got to the final line, which read, "You are my savior because you adopted me. Love, Jaclyn Hope."

I looked into her nine-year-old face and tried to find the words to refute these sentiments, but I was choked by my own emotions. As I opened my mouth to speak, she raised her hand, signaling me to stop. She looked into my eyes and said so quietly that only I could hear her words, "We both know the truth."

I did know the truth—that she could not be more wrong. It was she who'd saved me—from a life of complacency, a life of looking the other way.

The truth is, when you choose to love a child, you get back a million times what you give.

Parenting is the only job where success puts you out of business.

Even before I started mothering, I suspected that this might not be my easiest job. As a child, I couldn't stand cartoons, and I dreaded recess. How could I hope to be exuberant about them now? And as hard as I've tried, I often come up short. Eight-year-old Kate had to coach me before I was allowed to be the guest reader in her classroom. I unknowingly broke school policy on a field trip, which caused her untold embarrassment. I sweated buckets at a birthday party until the clown showed up.

One year on Mother's Day, eight-year-old Kate and six-year-old Jaclyn offered me homemade cards extolling their mother's virtues. Kate's card said she loved it when I made lasagna because that was her favorite food. I had no idea how to make lasagna, and if I had ever served it, it was Stouffers. I didn't even know lasagna was her favorite food.

Jaclyn's card said I was great at making scrambled eggs. That I can manage. But I winced when I thought back to my own childhood. We had a sit-down dinner in the dining room every evening, with all the food groups represented. Cloth napkins. Fancy gelatin salads served on decorative lettuce leaves. And birthday cakes that looked like carousels. And my mom never broke into a sweat at birthday celebrations, Halloween parties, or Brownie meetings.

Christy, at four, was too young to bestow a card with a written sentiment. But she offered up a prayer at bedtime instead. "Thank you, God, for my mommy. I really, really, really, really, really like her. And I love her! Amen."

I wanted to scream, à la Sally Field, "They like me! They really like me!" The truth was, they loved me in spite of all my inadequacies. They loved me because I was their mom. They loved me because I loved them and they knew it. It was that simple.

But, like all things, mothering has its own learning curve. I've definitely learned a few things along the way. Let me share some of them with you.

I've learned that mothers need a really good memory. You must be able to remember, with absolute clarity, who flipped the pancakes the last time you made them, whose turn it is to sit by the window when you get into the car, who got to water the flowers last, who talked to daddy on the phone first yesterday, and who got to open the door the last time the doorbell rang. Any slip-ups on these important scores and you will be subjected to the penalty of hysterical meltdowns and profuse crocodile tears.

I've learned that mothers need to have the precision and skill of a surgeon. If there is only one candy flower left on the three-day-old birthday cake, you'd better be able to precisely cut it into three exactly equal pieces without, God forbid, breaking it. And if, under the intense scrutiny of three sets of watching eyes, you lose your concentration and cause it to break, you'd better remember who had to eat the broken piece last time you messed up. (See previous paragraph.)

I've learned that there is such a thing as too much information. When my youngest child came to me and said, "Mom, I need a whole roll of paper towels," I naively asked why. Now, a few years older and wiser, I don't ask. I've got a fluorescent-green pig colored in permanent magic marker on my bathroom vanity to prove that there are some things you really don't want to know.

I've learned that a mother never has the last word. When Jaclyn was about eight, I discovered eleven small brown splotches on my bedroom ceiling. Unable to fathom how they could have gotten there, I asked my resident expert on all puzzling situations—Jaclyn—if she knew.

"Maybe someone jumped on the bed with Coke in her hand," she said innocently.

A few days later, Jaclyn was telling me what her home would look like when she grew up. "I will never get married, so I'll have the whole house to myself," she said with glee. "I'm going to have lots of rooms and four beds."

"Why do you need four beds?" I asked.

"I'll have bunk beds for my two babies I adopt from China. And one big bed for you to sleep on when you spend the night with me."

"That's only three. What's the fourth one for?"

Jaclyn gave me her "how sad that you are so slow" look. "For jump-ing on, of course!"

"Oh, good," I replied with a grin. "Then I'm going to jump on *your* bed with Coke in *my* hand and make brown spots on your ceiling."

Without missing a beat, Jaclyn replied, "At *my* house, I'll only give you Sprite!"

I've learned that there is no way to keep children completely safe. No mat-ter how vigilant you are, danger lurks everywhere. Every time I meet a parent whose child has been harmed, I know that there, but for the grace of God, go I. So I'm grateful for the guardian angels who somehow manage to keep up with these active little ones.

One such guardian angel whispered into my mother's ear one day and gave her bionic speed and strength. Though she'd just had a double hip replacement, she somehow managed to hurdle two giant rhodo-dendron bushes to save my child from drowning while my husband and I sat not three feet away, oblivious to the fact that she had slipped quietly into the pool.

Three days after I adopted Jaclyn, I lost her in a huge park in China. It must have been an angel who tapped me on the shoulder and pointed out where she was hiding, desperately trying to evade this stranger she was now supposed to call Mama.

I've learned that some of the biggest hurts children will suffer don't come from deeds, but from words. A mother's heart breaks at the hurtful words spoken to her children—the ones that shame them, that point out their imperfections. The ones masked behind teasing. The careless remarks that provoke heartbroken sobs. Such words hurt me even more than them. I marvel that anyone is able to traverse the path to adulthood when so many thoughtless remarks mar the way, cutting like glass into the essence of our beings.

I've learned that it is better to let children try to do something than to have it done "right." This was a tough one for a control freak like me. One year I actually snuck out under cover of darkness and planted my flowers by moonlight so I could avoid having three little helpers on this dirty job. I eventually changed my ways and allowed them to plant all the flowers themselves while I stayed inside and avoided giving advice. And if the neighbors shook their heads over the bright colors scattered around the yard and the fact that all the purple ones were bunched together, I couldn't care less. The smiles of triumph on three small faces meant more to me than any perfect garden could.

I've learned the importance of teaching children to pray. Because my own conversations with God have gotten me through so many difficult times, this was a given for me. I read a story once about someone who had a near-death experience. She likened prayer to beams of light that came forth from our hearts to the heavens. She spoke of different intensities of light and believed that the strongest beams came from mothers' prayers. I'm not so sure.

Cindy and the girls on Chinese New Year

Then let them teach you how to pray. Kate once prayed for the foster child of a family friend. She said, "Please, God, let Kristina know in her heart that a mom will get her and that all her empty spaces will then be filled with love." As I tucked her in, she chided me for failing to mention Kristina in my prayers.

"The truth is," I told her frankly, "I don't know how to pray for Kristina any more. I don't really believe that she's going to get a mom."

Kristina was one of the many children whom the system had failed. Our friends had tried to adopt her, but the courts returned her over and over again to a drug-addicted parent. Heartbroken, our friends had adopted another child. Now nine years old, Kristina was unlikely to find an adoptive family.

"Mom," Kate said gently, "if you don't know how to pray for someone, just ask God to watch over them."

I was floored; she was right.

Jaclyn's prayers inspired me too. She once told God, "And please bless all the animals, even the ones that bite." Given how many folks have snapped at me in my life, I guess that prayer works for people too.

I think even God needs encouragement now and then. Kate was thanking Him once for healing her sister, and she exuberantly exclaimed, "You tried Your hardest, God, and You did it! You're the greatest!"

After you've taught your children to pray, let them teach you how to pray.

I've learned that a mother needs to answer all her children's questions—even the tough ones. When my kids were young, I felt like I was trying to keep up with three short Jeopardy contestants all day. In exasperation once, I asked Jaclyn why she asked so many questions.

"Because I want to know why you do things," she said.

Because she was so unrelenting in her demands for the truth, I stopped trying to dodge her tough questions.

Sometimes she asks questions I'm afraid to hear the answers to. A few years ago, a family in our neighborhood adopted two toddlers from Russia. After several extremely difficult months, the exhausted mother considered relinquishing one of the children. Jaclyn was incensed; she loved these little ones dearly. One day Jaclyn marched up to the grandmother and asked, "Are you going to take care of Andrew and Katherine now?" She stood, feet firmly planted, staring into the grandmother's eyes. "Well? Who is going to be their mama?"

You go, girl, I thought. Sometimes people need to be held accountable for their behavior. We shouldn't flinch from saying the truth out loud.

I've learned the importance of teaching children that kindness matters. When Kate graduated from fifth grade, the kids were all allowed to sit together at the graduation ceremony, without parental supervision. One girl, who was not well liked by the other children, walked across the stage to the boos of several of her classmates. Kate was aghast. The minute the ceremony was over, she hurried over to the child who had been booed and put her arms around her, gave her a big hug, and told her how well she had done and how special she was. It was, without a doubt, the proudest moment of my life.

I've learned that sometimes, what is unsaid matters most. I want simple acts of kindness to be second nature to my girls. So I look for opportunities to let them experience the joy in giving. We've made Easter baskets filled with toiletries for the nursing home down the road. The kids have helped me pack boxes to send to their former orphanages. They often clamor to add some of their own possessions to the boxes.

I've shown them pictures of the children we sponsor through the Warm Blankets Orphan Care foundation and asked them to help me pray for them.

The trickier part is teaching them what giving from the heart means—how to give without any expectation of thanks or praise. So I made it into a game. We once snuck over to the widow's house across the street and left a bouquet of flowers. When she later asked us if we had any idea where they came from, we feigned puzzlement. That May, we bought a Mother's Day gift for our lonely neighbor, signed the card with her dog's name, and left it on her front porch.

I was never sure how much the kids understood what I was trying to teach them or whether they attributed it all to their parents' bonkers behavior.

Then one day Kate and I embarked on a secret mission. She agreed to take from her green plastic piggy bank all the money she had acquired in her eight years of life. The bank had no opening other than a slot in the top, so I took a large knife and cut the slot wider until the money could be poured out. Kate hid in the closet, away from the prying eyes of Jaclyn, to count her life savings. I watched her neatly stack her coins into piles. She then told me proudly, "All together, I have a hundred and thirty-seven dollars!" Without even taking a breath, she said, "Mommy, how much does it cost to sponsor an orphan?"

And then I knew she got it; she knew what really mattered in life.

I've learned that you can have success in mothering just by showing up and trying your best. Of course, just showing up means more to some kids than others.

One day, Jaclyn overheard me talking about a toddler in China who was being adopted by our friends. The child was left on a bench in an amusement park with a bottle of milk and a box of biscuits. An elderly woman heard her crying and took her to the police station.

I didn't know Jaclyn had heard any of this. I tried to never speak of abandonment around her. She had her own painful memories, and it was still a topic too traumatic to speak of. But that night at bedtime, she told God, "Thank You for the grandma who found baby Grace and took her to the police. Her mom should have taken her there herself if she couldn't take care of her, but she didn't." She peeked one eye open and asked, "Mama, did the old lady find her in the daytime or in the dark?" When I told her the child was found during the day, she added, "And thank You, God, that baby Grace did not have to wait in the cold or the dark."

After she finished her prayer, she looked at me and whispered, "You wouldn't leave me on a bench, would you?"

I had repeatedly spoken reassurances to her in the years since her adoption, and it had been a long time since she'd asked for confirmation that I would be there for her. So I decided, just this once, to make light of it.

"Jaclyn, you know I would never, *ever* leave you anywhere. You, on the other hand, will probably grow up and leave *me* parked on a bench. I can see it now. You'll drive off in that pink convertible you always talk about, and you'll go off to the mall with your friends and leave me behind without a backward glance."

"Don't worry, Mama," Jaclyn said with a giggle. "I'll get a backseat just for you!'"

And that's the reward in motherhood. If you love your children with your whole heart and soul, if you survive all their questions, and if you somehow succeed in teaching them a few valuable lessons along the way, then one day you too may be relegated to the backseat.

Someone I once knew very well has disappeared.

It is impossible for me to remember who I was before I was a mother. The young woman who cared deeply about what she wore to a party has been replaced by someone who makes sure her girls are the ones with new dresses. The lady who relished the freedom to take a long bath without a parade of interruptions is gone too. The one who could stay up late and sleep in as long as she wanted on a Saturday morning—no remnant of her remains. And I thank God for that. Because there is no comparison between what I traded away and what I got in return. I gave myself to my children. And in return, I found myself.

Parenting is an amazing gift. It comes wrapped in childhood silliness. It comes sprinkled with magic moments. It comes tied with ribbons of joy. It is full of sticky fingers and soft, sleepy heads and sometimes sorrow that can't be hugged away. When our kids are little, it feels like forever until they'll be grown. And then forever is gone in a blink and you watch, teary-eyed, as they graduate. Parenting is a gift to be cherished and savored and then remembered fondly when the children are grown and live far away.

There is no adventure greater than the one you will find when you grab the hand of a child. Parenting surely is the most joyous, the most exhilarating, and the most exhausting of all life's gifts.

The Sixth Gift

Promise and Promises

The word promise has two separate and distinct meanings. One is that promise is the basis of our expectations, the indication of something favorable to come. In Michigan where we endure endless winters, the first tiny bud brings with it the promise of spring. The promise of the future is enveloped in our hope that good things lie ahead.

The more common use of the word promise is to signify a vow. In many ways, our lives are shaped by our promises. We promise ourselves to another forever, and a marriage is made. We promise to keep confidences, and a friendship is formed. We promise to work hard, and a job is secured.

But a broken promise can be life changing. We break our vows, and a marriage is over. We share a secret given to us in trust, and a friendship is derailed. We fail to honor our commitments at work, and we face the door.

And what about the promises we make to ourselves? The hidden vows and the "never agains" that we speak of to no one. We all have them, and they can be the greatest motivators in our choices. I made more than my share when I was younger. I failed miserably at most of them.

My mother made many unspoken promises. She gave up a career she loved in order to be a homemaker. It was the 1960s;

there were no choices for women, only expectations. She spent her days devoted to the care of four children and a husband. She cooked and cleaned and did laundry and baked and ran errands and chauffeured us kids endlessly. She was a Brownie leader, a Sunday school teacher, a PTA member, and a volunteer. If she ever sat down with a mug of coffee and the *Reader's Digest*, it would be for the briefest of interludes before someone needed her for something, and she'd spring back into service, pushing down a deep sigh. She had no "Girls Night Out" or luncheons with friends. She agonized over every dime she spent on herself. She returned the fur coat my dad gave her and used the money to get the portable TV we kids wanted. We never thanked her.

I came of age at the height of the women's movement. I watched my mother's life, and I promised myself I would never be her. Little did I realize that I could never be her. The selflessness, the devotion, the giving of her life to others—it wasn't in me. And the ultimate irony is that I now desperately wish I could be more like her.

After college I promised myself that I'd make important life decisions by carefully weighing the pros and cons as I'd been taught in business school. At the time, I didn't understand that all really important decisions in life need to be made with the heart.

After working for years, I got fed up with lousy bosses and tired of being treated as an underling. I promised myself I would one day be in a position of authority and leadership. I had no idea that a far greater reward is found in service to others.

I promised myself I'd have just one child so I could remain fully engaged in the career I had worked so hard for. I abandoned that promise the minute I figured out that holding my paycheck paled in comparison to holding my baby.

I promised myself I'd never use TV as a babysitter or give my kids junk food or let them crawl into my bed at night. Amazing how quickly those promises fell apart. Endless loops of Barney were a small price to pay for fifteen minutes to mop the kitchen floor. Watching the delight on their faces as they licked ice cream cones toppled my concerns about sugar. And holding their sleepy bodies against mine when the boogie monster scared them into my bed was not the sacrifice I thought it would be, but the purest joy imaginable.

After being dumped by my first love, I promised myself I would never be hurt by love again. But the price that promise extracted was too high. It meant I would never fully open my heart. The day I abandoned that promise by giving myself completely to another was the happiest day of my life.

I promised myself I'd have money in the bank and an investment portfolio that reflected aggressive savings and judicious spending. I realize now that true wealth has nothing to do with bank accounts and everything to do with how much we love and how much we are loved by others.

Now I think of the promises I should have made:

To embrace learning.

To work hard.

To try.

To refuse to live in fear.

To never stop believing in the goodness of others.

To be kind.

To not live with blinders on.

To be joyful.

To not look back with regret but to look forward with hope.

The best is still ahead.

The summer the girls turned four, six, and eight, I planned several family excursions. I'd learned the hard way to limit these trips to no more than long weekends—there was, after all, only so many continuous days any adult could be expected to share a tiny hotel room with three small children. I had found that three nights in a row was about the maximum I could do without threats of serious bodily harm.

Of course, any trip provided opportunities to see and hear amazing things. Ours did not disappoint. As we were traveling to Amish Acres in Indiana for three fun-filled days of gawking at Amish people, we passed a large cone-shaped storage facility holding road salt.

"Look, there's a volcano," shrieked Jaclyn. Guess we didn't have to take the kiddies to Hawaii after all.

Later that summer, we headed out to the Michigan State Fair. On the drive there, I told the girls my favorite sight at the fair was always the huge mother pig and her newborn litter.

"Animals are disgusting," Jaclyn said.

"Why do you think that?" I asked.

"The teachers taught us that at school. They showed us a movie where a giraffe stuck his tongue into his nose and then put it in his mouth." Jaclyn grimaced. "Then Jason showed the class how he could do the same thing!"

In spite of Jaclyn's disgust, I was excited to see that pigs were the first exhibit inside the front gate. I ushered the kids inside, even though Christy refused to stop plugging her nose. Our attention was immediately drawn to a display I can only describe as a loud, aggressive brawl between two huge hogs. I was riveted to this horrific display until Jaclyn jabbed me in the side and demanded, "Why did you bring us here?" Good question.

Trips provided us with amazing things to hear too. One morning at a restaurant, I ordered six-year-old Jaclyn's usual breakfast.

"No sausage today, Mama," Jaclyn announced. "I'm a vegetarian." She remained firmly rooted to this position . . . until lunchtime.

We took lots of little road trips, which gave me ample opportunities to practice my least-developed skill: driving in terrible traffic when I have absolutely no idea where I'm going. I am impaired even driving in the city where I've lived all my life.

The only reassuring part of this is that I have several girlfriends who are similarly impaired. All lifelong residents of Detroit, we have had brunch regularly at the same restaurant for over twenty years. Yet none of us can find it without asking the others for as-sistance. One of these ladies is a top business executive with an MBA from Harvard. When my Chinese immigrant friend, Fong, got up the courage to learn to drive in the United States, she told me, "When I find the road I'm looking for, I feel so lucky!" I reassured her that was exactly how I felt.

I prepared myself ahead of time for our family's first trip of the summer in 2002. I got turn-by-turn directions from Mapquest. They failed to mention, however, that the only road that led to where we were going was closed for construction. Complicat-ing this was the fact that my dear husband had to make a quick conference call to some very important clients on the drive. This short call lasted *an hour and twenty minutes.*

The minute Rick got on the phone with his clients, Jaclyn pulled out her secret stash of potato chips and started eating them with great fanfare in front of her sisters. This led to howling pro-tests, which I desperately tried to shush. I hissed at Jaclyn that she needed to share. Reluctantly, she broke off microscopic pieces of potato chips for each sister while stuffing full-sized chips into her mouth. This fueled Kate's anger, and her voice quickly escalated into the battle chant "I'm telling Mom! I'm telling Mom!" I was sitting less than eight inches away. Did they think I didn't hear?

My husband glared at me while covering the mouthpiece on his phone. Clearly, *I* was the problem.

The potato chip war escalated until it was suddenly silenced by an unforeseen consequence. Jaclyn got carsick. This added a fun new dimension to the drive. I was in a construction zone, with no place to pull over, while groping in the backseat in a futile attempt to wipe up vomit.

This gave Jaclyn the idea for a new game: Try to Gross Out Your Sister by Showing Her the Barf. This was highly successful. Kate soon began to gag. I was almost ready to vomit myself! I rolled down the car window to get some fresh air, which resulted in a wailing cry from Christy, who did *not* want the window down.

During my husband's "short little phone call," I managed to get hopelessly lost on the back roads of rural Indiana. Rick gestured that I should pull over and ask for directions. I stopped at the only building in sight—a hardware store with a sign on the door that read "Ran to the bank. Be back in 20 minutes." Two old-timers stood at the corner, so I approached them, hoping they could direct me to the road I needed.

"We'll, let's see," the first man said. "You go down this road here till you get to the yellow fence. You turn right there and go down past the Speedway till you see the new library. Hey, Hank, have you seen that new library yet?" This query digressed into a sales pitch on the wonders of this new literary establishment.

Meanwhile, Rick continued to talk on the phone, and the children grimaced at me from the backseat.

Finally noticing my impatience, the old man returned to the task at hand. "You turn left at the library—not sure what that road is called—then head southwest for about two miles. You'll see two big red barns right next to each other. That's where you want to turn left." He droned on and on while I nodded politely, wishing I had a pen and paper to write all this down.

Cindy and the girls on the roller coaster at Wonderland

The second man interrupted. "Well, that might be the *easiest* way, but I know a faster way." He gave equally convoluted directions.

Now thoroughly confused, I thanked the men and slunk back to my car. I drove off, seething with frustration, shooting daggers at my husband, who was still on his "short phone call."

A few yards down the road, Rick covered the phone and whispered, "Look out for the geese!" He frantically pointed to a gaggle of about fifteen geese standing smack dab in the middle of the road.

I slammed on the brakes and shouted at my "helpful" husband, "Do you think I'm Mr. Magoo? How could I possibly miss fifteen geese right in front of the car?"

"I'm sure my clients enjoyed that," he hissed in an angry stage whisper.

Finally spotting a gas station, I went inside to ask for directions. The woman working the register followed me outside. "See that red car?" she asked. I nodded. "Follow it, and turn right at the light." Now *that* I could do. If only I'd asked a woman the first time.

For me, it was a summer filled with lessons learned. I learned how frustrating and frazzling "fun" family times can be. I learned that a GPS system is really the best invention of the last century. I learned to lower my expectations around any trip that involved small children.

But I also learned something else that summer that I'll never forget. In fact, when I heard the words spoken by Jaclyn, they stopped me in my tracks. It happened later in that summer when we visited an amusement park in Toronto. It was quite chilly that day, and a cold drizzle fell intermittently. The kids were thrilled because that meant the lines were short. But by the end of the day, I was miserable. My entire body ached, and I could feel a head cold coming on. I had gamely ridden the roller coasters with Kate, and the muscles in my neck were stiff from trying to keep my head from popping off on the turns.

As we headed toward the car, I surreptitiously ran my tongue over my teeth to make sure that they were all still in place after all the jarring from the rides. Chilled to the bone, I slid inside the minute the doors unlocked.

"Oh, Mom," Kate said, "this has been the best day of my life!"

Instantly, the chill was gone. My body no longer ached. Even my neck felt better as I basked in the glow of my daughter's excitement.

Not one to leave well enough alone, I asked Jaclyn, "Was this the best day of your life too?"

"No," she replied.

"Well, what's the best day of *your* life then?"

"Tomorrow," she said quietly.

Her response took my breath away; I wondered why things that totally escaped me were always so crystal clear to Jaclyn. Why did I spend so much time looking back, chewing on regret, beating myself up over things left undone? If you live in a state of expectation, the best is always ahead . . . wrapped in the promise of tomorrow.

Promise is potential undiscovered.

During my years as an adoption social worker, I learned that international adoption is not for the faint of heart. It's complicated, expensive, and emotionally exhausting. But I came to love the adoptive families I worked with. Each had a unique story about how and why they had made this choice for their family. The stories were all different, but the motive was always the same: they had love to give, and they wanted a child to share in that love.

I will never forget the Davis family. Pam and her husband, Mike, already had five sons. For most, that would be more than enough children. But they desperately wanted a daughter to add to the mix. Pam confided to me that she was sure the reason none of her biological children had been a girl was because they were destined to adopt. Deeply religious, they believed that everything works together for good. They held to a firm faith that the child who was destined to be their daughter was going to come to them in a different way.

When I visited their home to do the required inspection, I laughed with Pam at the bedroom setup. The boys all shared one bedroom that they called "the bunk house," as it held bunk beds and trundles. Across the hall was another large bedroom with a bay window and a walk-in closet. That room was decorated in a princess theme—all pink and white and filled with frilly girl things. The closet was jammed with pink dresses and sparkly shoes and sequined purses that would make any little girl swoon. All they needed was the princess.

Because international adoption is a lengthy process, it was nearly a year later when Pam and Mike returned from their adoption trip to China. Pam told me, in a worried voice, that she thought something was wrong with the long-awaited princess they had named Amanda. I reassured Pam that most children have developmental delays after they are adopted, but that time and love and exercise and good nutrition generally resolve those issues in a short time period. I had worked with nearly a hundred international adoptees, and with the exception of my own daughter, none of these children had had any long-lasting physical problems.

I urged Pam to trust her instincts, but her doubts lingered. After lots of medical tests and consultations, she received the diagnosis that Amanda had mild cerebral palsy. I swallowed hard when she told me that. I knew firsthand how hard it was to hear news like this. But Pam assured me that she and Mike loved Amanda with their whole hearts and believed she was destined to be a member of their family. She emphatically stated that they would have adopted her even if they had known of her disability ahead of time.

In many ways, Amanda had found the perfect family for her. Pam was determined to find the best therapies for her child, and Mike was a doctor. And five big brothers clamored for the chance to carry Amanda in their arms when she labored to crawl.

There are no promises in life. There are no promises in parenting. But every child holds promise.

Fast forward eight years. As victims of the horrific economic downturn in Detroit, my husband and I had been taking turns commuting back and forth between his job in Chicago and my job in Detroit for more than three years. I had tried every possible travel arrangement to avoid my every-other-weekend car ride that was a twelve-hour round trip. The train was constantly late, often bringing me back at one a.m. when I had to get up for work less than five hours later. The merger of the two major airlines serving Detroit had added more delays and cost and frustration.

On one trip, I sat at the Chicago airport for nearly five hours waiting for a fifty-minute flight. Adding insult to injury, I was forced to surrender my carry-on bag and have it checked. I arrived at the Detroit airport late on a Sunday night in an exceptionally crabby mood.

I stood at baggage claim, waiting for the notoriously slow luggage handlers to unload the flight. When the conveyer finally began to move, stacks of suitcases jammed the chute. Passengers groaned. It would take forever to get someone from the airline to untangle this mess.

I was exhausted and irritated and feeling sorry for myself. How could I keep doing this? I was trapped by my circumstances, trapped by my house that was worth less than what I owed on it, and things seemed to be getting worse. But there was no way out.

Glancing around, I noticed a small knot of people with banners welcoming home a missionary who was returning from overseas. I spotted a beautiful Asian girl in their midst who looked to be about nine years old. She was surrounded by older boys. One of them yelled, "Come on, Amanda, let's run."

Amanda? I looked again at the beautiful smiling girl running to catch up to her brothers. I swiveled around and saw Pam in the crowd. I rushed toward her. She gave me a big hug and explained that Amanda had had intensive therapy, including everything medical science could offer and something that medical science couldn't offer: a family's unfailing love and support. She had beaten the odds.

Pam called Amanda over and explained, "This is the lady who helped us bring you here from China."

Amanda flashed me a brilliant smile and, without any coaching, gave me a big hug and whispered, "Thank you."

My exhaustion and sadness were replaced with a grin I could not wipe off my face. Discouragement had been replaced with unexpected joy. I felt as if God had reached down and literally sent me a hug.

We listen to prognoses and dire predictions and expect the worst to happen. We feel trapped by the circumstances of our lives. But every now and then, we beat the odds.

We don't really know the promise in others. We don't even know the promise in ourselves. Sometimes it takes the dark moments to reveal the light of our true potential. And a flickering glimpse of that promise can fuel our hopes for tomorrow.

It all begins with a promise.

Because Jaclyn was four when we adopted her from China, I understood that she would be scared at the prospect of leaving behind all that was familiar to her. In an effort to prepare her, I sent her a package, in care of the orphanage. It contained a teddy bear that proudly wore the American flag on his sweater— I hoped it would comfort her and also symbolize her new life. I put some girly hair bows in the box and also tucked inside a small Mickey Mouse photo album. Inside the album I had placed carefully chosen pictures of our family and what was to be her new home. I asked my Chinese friend Fong to label each picture so that a member of the orphanage staff could help prepare her for what was ahead.

The teddy bear was unable to provide much comfort. As the children were not allowed to own anything in the orphanage—even clothes, shoes, and underwear were shared—she was not given the teddy bear until she was loaded into the car on her way to meet us. But she never had much inter-

Jaclyn in the orphanage studying the photo book of her soon-to-be adoptive family

est in the bear anyway. She wasn't used to sleeping with a stuffed animal. Her nighttime comfort came from the clenched hand of her orphanage charge, Xiao Xiao, who slept in the bed next to her. Given what nighttime was like in the orphanage, the grasp of another's hand was barely enough to squelch the terror. A teddy bear would not have been up to this monumental task.

Jaclyn's hair was crudely shorn when we met her—a preventive measure to keep head lice from spreading among the orphanage children—so the hair bows were useless too. But she clutched the photo album to her at our first meeting. Each day on the adoption trip in China, Jaclyn and I spent time studying those pictures as I tried valiantly to say the Chinese words for "big sister," "little sister," and "your home." The photo book represented my promise to her—a new life—and she desperately clung to that promise. It was later obvious how carefully she had studied those pictures.

When we arrived home from China, she pointed out to me some details in our house—drapes, a chair—and showed me that they didn't quite match the pictures in the photo book.

Several months later she came to me frantic because she couldn't find the Mickey Mouse photo book. I had almost forgotten it, but the intensity of her search made me join her in it. We discovered it behind other books in her book shelf.

She opened the book and showed me some pictures that puzzled her. One was of our family sitting on the hood of a car at Universal Studios in Florida. "Where's that car?" she asked.

I explained that the picture had been taken on a family vacation.

"Oh," she said with annoyance. "It's not fair you had fun without Jaclyn."

I tried to explain that she wasn't in our family when we took that trip, but she was not mollified. She added it to her ever-growing list of things in life that were not fair.

"You have to take me there now," she insisted, "just me, so I can have as much fun as Kate and Christy."

I told her that wasn't possible. She became quiet, slowly turning the pages of the book with a faraway look in her eyes.

I gently asked, "Jaclyn, do you remember when they gave you the photo book at the orphanage?"

"Yes," she said thoughtfully. "They let me show it to my friends on the day I found my mama."

"What did your friends say?"

"They say, 'Oh! So beautiful! So beautiful!'"

"What did they think was so beautiful? Was it your new home? Your new bedroom?"

She looked at me as if the answer was obvious. "No. They say my new *mama* so beautiful."

I could hardly enjoy this sweet compliment. How could I not have realized that, for these children, material things would pale in comparison to the riches of having a mother?

"I show the book to Jin Xun Li," Jaclyn continued. "She say, 'I wish I could have a mama too.'" Then she added, "I show this book to my baby, Xiao Xiao. He ask me over and over and over, 'I see again?'" She gave a little chuckle of annoyance as only those who have cared for a persistent toddler can understand.

"Then he say, 'Jiao, Jiao, can I come live with you?'" Her eyes filled with tears at the memory. "He wanted me to *promise*. But I didn't promise." She couldn't promise. She had no idea what would become of her or how far away America was. She'd also had two adoptions fall through before we adopted her. She knew that false hope had the power to devastate more than anything else in the dark place where they lived.

But a promise was made. She made a sacred vow, deep in her soul, that she would help her dear charge, Xiao Xiao, "find a mama." And she was true to her word. Her relentless advocacy for him, combined with a series of small miracles, resulted in his adoption by Jaclyn's aunt just fifteen months after she had left him. When Jaclyn marched back into that orphanage and claimed him, he grabbed her hand—trusting completely.

And it all began with a promise.

The promises we make to ourselves shape our destiny. The promises that others make to us shape our trust—in the future, in the goodness of people, in our tenacious belief that the best is ahead. Sometimes all we have to hold on to is a promise and the hope it brings—and that promise can be one of the greatest gifts of life.

The Seventh Gift

Pathways and Possibilities

If you had told me years ago that I'd visit orphanages in a third-world country on multiple occasions, I would have laughed out loud. If you'd told me I would one day leave a chunk of my heart on the other side of this earth, I would have scoffed. If you had said I would someday write a book, I wouldn't have believed it. If you'd told me I would speak on TV, radio, and every other venue I could find on behalf of family-less children, I would have shaken my head in incredulity. If you had predicted that I would have my life transformed by a child's truth, I would have turned away.

When I graduated from college with a business major, I had a clear picture of my future. I wanted to make money. Lots of it. I would have a successful career and live in a nice suburban home. Success for me was family, a great job, close friends, and good health. And plenty of nice stuff. You know—an ordinary life.

But two intersections changed the path of my life forever. The first was meeting Jaclyn. When I adopted her at the age of four, she constantly reminded me of where she'd been and what she had suffered. She would not let me forget those she'd left behind in the orphanage. She spoke often of the huge chasm between the "haves" and the "have nots" in this world. She made me see that I could not turn my back and pretend that suffering didn't exist. Her vision opened my eyes.

This led to the second thing that changed my path forever—choosing to see with my heart. Our hearts allow us to push ahead when our minds tell us otherwise. The heart doesn't accept that nothing can be done to right a wrong. Our hearts don't stop praying for miracles. Our hearts never stop believing.

Our possibilities expand and contract in proportion to our love. The most satisfying path in life is the one lit by love. And finally finding our way is one of the true gifts of life.

> In encouraging our children to find
> their own path, we must let go when our
> heart is most desperate to hold on.

Almost before I knew it, it was time for my youngest child, Christy, to begin kindergarten. I can still remember the day vividly for one reason: it was the worst day of my life. When her father, Rick, saw my stricken face, he chided me. "She's ready for this—don't let her see how upset you are. She had to grow up sometime. You knew she wouldn't stay a baby forever." When I had talked of home schooling her, he thought I was kidding. Now, seeing my tear-stained face, he wasn't so sure.

I looked at him miserably, unable to articulate what was upsetting me. It wasn't that I knew school would take away her innocence. And it would. There she would learn that magic doesn't exist and that wishes coming true is make-believe. She would learn that Santa Claus and fairies and all the other fantasies of childhood are merely smoke and mirrors. And that danger lurked around every corner. They would do such a good job of teaching her to be afraid, she would have terror-filled dreams of strangers abducting her just because an elderly lady said hello to her at the bus stop.

It wasn't that I was worried about vying for placement in her heart with her new teacher. I knew her teacher would be quoted like Solomon and that she would be imitated and admired like no other. I had seen this before with her older sisters and was glad Christy would have someone so special in her life.

I wasn't afraid of what she would learn. I knew that in addition to the alphabet and multiplication tables, she would learn at school that she was different. She would be teased for a multitude of things, from the color of her gym shoes to the shape of her eyes. She would learn to shield her soul from the barbs of others. We all must learn eventually to build walls around our fragile hearts. She, like the rest of us, would one day need them.

It wasn't that I feared for her safety. Even though she could barely climb the bus steps, she would be changing schools in the middle of the day and eating lunch with no one to tell her she must finish her sandwich before she ate her pudding. But I trusted the school system. So far they hadn't lost any kids; I knew they would watch out for mine too.

It wasn't that I felt like my life would flounder,

Christy on her first day of kindergarten

have a rudderless sense of purposelessness to it, without her to guide. I'd always had myriad interests and more work to do than time to do it in. Motherhood was not the only thing that defined me, just the biggest thing right now. And to be honest, it would be a small relief to let go of some of that awesome responsibility.

It wasn't that I knew she would suddenly go from being the center of my universe to being one small star in a sky filled with constellations. To the people at school, she would be ordinary— with her own idiosyncrasies, but still much like all the others. To me, she was extraordinary—not at all like the others. Not even close. But I knew how warped she might become if she was not made to understand that the world did not revolve around her. So I was ready for others to judge her, assess her, and see her differently than I did.

It wasn't for any of the usual reasons.

The only way I could explain it was by remembering how I felt in those first few weeks after I gave birth to Kate. I recalled the sadness I felt when I realized my womb, so recently full of life, was now empty. I remember pushing my floppy, air-filled abdomen and mourning the loss of that little person who had filled me. Yes, now I could hold her in my arms, but that was the beginning of the eventual separation of her and me. She no longer went everywhere with me. She did not lull me to sleep with her gentle movements. She did not make me smile with the rhythm of her hiccups. She was no longer my secret—the one I kept to myself for so long, hoarding my joy until my bulging belly betrayed me. We were once one, and now we were two, and the reality of that change made me sad. My body seemed to have lost its purpose. Now it was an empty shell, where once it had held the most precious gift of life.

This was the reason I was sad. Kindergarten represented the beginning of the separation of Christy and me. Although she had never lived in my body, this little one had filled my heart and soul like no other. She and I were like one being.

I was worried about what would be left of me when she was fully grown and off beginning her own life. Whose smile would I savor upon waking? Whose needs would transcend my own? How would I sleep knowing she was not tucked away safely under my roof? Who would call to me in the night for comfort? Who would bury her sweet body against mine when she was tired? Who would gently kiss my palm and then tuck my fingers around the spot to protect this special kiss? Who would tell me, after the briefest absence, that she missed me so much her tummy ached? When she left home, I was afraid my heart would mirror that empty, lifeless womb. It would be stretched out and vacant. And even if, in time, it shrank back to its former size, it would never feel full again. *Who would I be when the best part of me was gone?*

Once the school bus had pulled away with my precious child inside and I knew she couldn't see my tears, I laid my head down on the steering wheel of the car and sobbed. Rick drove by the bus stop and found me parked there. When he saw the depths of my grief, he stopped chiding me.

"I have to go," I said as I rolled up the car window. "I want to make sure I'm there when the bus arrives at school so I can help her find her classroom." I took a few minutes to wipe away the trail left by my tears and then drove away. I was sure Rick was shaking his head in puzzlement after witnessing what he must have believed was some hysterical, irrational moment from his otherwise mostly sane wife.

I stood at the school waiting for Christy, feeling more alone and miserable than I had ever felt in my life. The bus finally arrived and Christy got off, concentrating on mastering the huge last step without stumbling. I reached out, and Christy grabbed my hand. Then she marched proudly into her new school. I showed her where to hang her backpack and introduced her to a classmate who had just been adopted from Kazakhstan and whose mother was struggling to trust this new school with her precious child who could not understand the new language. Christy took the child's hand. After I encouraged her several times to sit, she willed her nervous legs to bend underneath her and looked up anxiously at her new teacher.

As reluctant as I was to turn around, there was nothing left to do but go. I turned my back and walked alone to the parking lot, trying desperately to remember who I was before I was a mother. It was strange to remember that I had actually felt whole back then. Now something within me was missing when my children weren't with me.

Before you become a parent, everyone warns you that your life will never be the same. I accepted the endless laundry, the chaos, the sticky messes, the dirty diapers, the racket, the carpools, and the Brownie meetings. They were a small price to pay for the joy, the love, the touch of tiny fingers.

What they don't tell you is that your heart will never be the same. That your children will claim it and never let it go. And that absolutely nothing would be big enough to fill the void when they find their own path.

We all owe a debt of gratitude to the ones who lit our path until we could clearly see our own possibilities.

I'd like to say that I always encouraged my children to think big. That I told them to reach for the stars. That I ran beside them, cheering them on, as they made all their dreams come true. But it isn't true. Maybe because I don't have any special talents. Maybe because I didn't know how to dream big. Maybe because I was afraid of their failure and disappointment.

When my oldest, Kate, came to me when she was in fourth grade and said she wanted to run for student council, I asked how many other kids were running. "My whole class," she said. I tried to prepare her not to be disappointed if she lost. She won.

Two years later she tried out for the middle-school musical *The Music Man*. Thanks to having a tone-deaf mother, she had no musical background. I reminded her that only a handful of sixth graders were cast in parts and that she'd be competing with kids who'd had singing and dance lessons. She got a part. When she gave me the news, she asked me point blank, "Why do you try to snatch all my dreams?"

It's true. I was a dream snatcher. And I determined to change. Luckily, she had other adults who were influential in helping her see her own possibilities. Chief among them was a remarkable woman named Mrs. Vogel, Kate's middle-school teacher.

When you talk to people who have dreamed big dreams and succeeded, it's interesting to note how many times the encouragement of a great teacher fueled their ambition. With gratitude for what Mrs. Vogel had done for my daughter and many others, I wrote to her:

Dear Mrs. Vogel,

When the curtain opened and I saw Kate on stage, I almost didn't recognize her as my daughter. What happened to the eleven-year-old girl I gave you? How did you transform her into a young woman whose beauty and poise nearly took my breath away? The tilt of her head, the subtleties of her gestures, the exuberance of her song—where did that come from?

She asked me before the performance if I would start the standing ovation when the show ended. Start it? In the first ten minutes of the first act, I had to suppress the urge to stand on my chair and applaud. I saw, maybe for the first time, someone unknown to me—and what she could be.

When she first mentioned her interest in trying out for the play, I was surprised. At her age, I would never have done anything to distinguish myself in any way from my peers. I wanted to hide from the spotlight, not be in it. But she is not me.

She hung in there, even when all her friends backed out before try-outs. She was thrilled to be chosen for a part in the chorus. When I asked her if she felt bad that her part wasn't bigger, she looked at me in surprise. "Mom," she said patiently, "if it weren't for the townspeople, there wouldn't be a town. And if there wasn't a town, there wouldn't be a need for the Music Man. Get it?" I got it. She added quietly, "Besides, it's not about the size of the part; it's about how much fun we're going to have! I get to sing and dance and act. What could be better than that?" Indeed.

I was not one of the parents who volunteered to help. This did not show a lack of desire on my part to be helpful—it reflected my sheer terror at the implications. When I came into that rehearsal room, I saw crowds of kids giggling and telling secrets and fooling around and moving in an endless mass of confusion in every possible direction. What you saw was possibility.

I saw you run the same scenes over and over, endlessly correcting and guiding and instructing and redoing. All the while you were expected to keep an eye on those not on stage, making sure they were where they were supposed to be and not getting into too much trouble or making too much noise. Time and time again, with little apparent frustration, you brought them back on task. You directed them, and you never lost it. You showed patience.

When I opened the program and read Kate's bio, I was immediately struck by thoughts of her dreams for her future. When she discusses her goals with me, the possibilities are conventional and easily within her reach. But with you, she shared her secret desires and dreams that would make her stretch. When she saw herself through the lens of your encouragement, the possibilities grew. You saw potential.

I am ashamed that people don't do more to thank teachers for all they do. You teach math and science and social studies and reading and everything else in the curriculum. But the reality runs much deeper than the complexities of algebraic equations and the subtleties of literature. We expect you to also teach our children to handle all the changes that being a teenager brings with it and how to build lasting friendships and how to resist temptation. We expect you to not only be a role model but also a provider of guidance and support. We expect you to keep them on course and safe and focused. And if you ever fail at any of these, we are quick to complain, to go to the principal and speak critically of you. We justify our behavior because we have entrusted you with the most precious thing in our world—our children. And because we give you our children, we expect a great deal in return. You can't fail at this—the stakes are too high. Yet we never come in just to say, "Thank you."

Today I would like to say thank you.

Thank you for the endless months of rehearsals you orchestrated. Thank you for the hours you spent planning and choreographing and making sure every detail was attended to. Thank you for bringing your love with you to work. Because no one would have done what you did for the money.

Thank you for taking a group of kids who are mature and immature, shy and loud, talented and spirited, rowdy and thoughtful, and making a cast and crew out of them. Thank you for looking at our kids and seeing possibilities.

Thank you for making it about fun and camaraderie and supporting each other. Thanks for showing them that all the pieces are needed to make the whole remarkable. Thank you for helping them understand that it is about the experience, not about one person's share of the applause.

Thank you for the gift of seeing our children as actors and dancers and singers and technicians. Thank you for letting them try on new roles and encouraging them to work together. Thank you for helping us to see them in new ways.

Thank you for teaching them not only the lessons in books, but lessons about life as well.

Most of all, thank you for teaching them how to dream.

With admiration and respect,
Cindy Champnella (a.k.a. Kate's mom)

Mrs. Vogel was stunned by my letter. I was stunned to learn that no one, in the thirty years in which she had given herself to children, had ever really thanked her.

There are two ways to thank those who show us our possibilities and guide us on the path toward them. One is by actually saying, "Thank you." Not a cursory "Thanks." A look-you-in-the-eyes-and grab-your-hand-and speak-from-the heart "Thank you." The other is by supporting others who are pursuing their dreams. It's a pay-it-forward kind of thinking, because there really is no way to pay back those who can glimpse our possibilities when we ourselves can't see them clearly. Except by becoming a dream maker.

We can choose our path, but sometimes our path chooses us.

I am not a writer. Chances are good that you have never before come across that admission in any book that you are reading. But in my case, it is the truth. I went to business school after graduating from college, and when that career path proved less than satisfying, I got a second graduate degree in psychology. I took the minimum number of English courses required and avoided writing classes like the plague. I don't like to write. It wasn't a path I would ever have pursued. The only thing I like less than writing is public speaking and promotion and asking strangers to buy something—like my book.

So how did I end up on a path so different from the one I began on?

After I adopted Jaclyn and she began telling me who she was, I found myself overwhelmed by pain. The horror this brave little soul had endured by the time she became my daughter was unthinkable. I often thought that if I gave in to the sadness I felt about what she had been through, my tears would have no end. I needed to share my hurt; I could not hold it in. But I was a busy mom of three small children who also held down a demanding job as a school adminis-trator. There was no time in my world for long heart-to-heart talks with supportive friends. There was no time or money for therapy. Even my mom only had only so much capacity to listen.

So I utilized technology to recapture the coffee-klatch close-ness that homemakers had in the past—I e-mailed a small group of friends, nearly daily, about Jaclyn. What she told me. What she had suffered. What she had borne witness to. What she would not let me forget. I wrote of her pain and her adjustment and her courage and her never-ending advocacy to be reunited with the child she had left behind in the orphanage.

Sharing with this small group of friends, many who lived far away, was my attempt to keep my perspective, and oftentimes to gain perspective, as I broached the challenge of becoming a mother to this challenging four-year-old who had claimed my heart. The circle of people following Jaclyn's story dramatically expanded. Several people asked if they could share Jaclyn's anec-dotes with groups they were involved in. Some did not ask, but simply forwarded my messages to their families and friends.

Within six months, I began getting letters from people all over the United States, telling me that Jaclyn, or some aspect of her story, had touched their hearts or lives. The circle continued to grow. It soon contained people who had no interest in adop-tion themselves but had begun to love Jaclyn. Friends told me of the keen disappointment of others in their circle when I didn't write. Two women wrote to me from Paris telling me they were "Jaclyn fans." Some of my e-mails were picked up in publications and newsletters all over the United States.

And still the e-mails came. I was invited to speak to various groups about adoption. Hoping to touch hearts and interest others, I accepted these invitations, forgetting for the moment that I had no abilities in the area of public speaking. I was amazed at how many times people from the audience came up to me afterward and asked, "Are you Jaclyn's mom?" Then they would tell me they were following her story through connections to people I often did not even know. I wondered if others would be touched by it, inspired by her life and changed, in some small way, by hearing her truth.

It's a huge thing to ask a child to share her story—especially one as painful as this one. To make public your most private hurts—is it ever fair to ask that of a child, even if the intention is a good one? I needed her permission. I needed her commitment. I needed her unwavering support. Jaclyn and I talked about the impact that sharing her story could have on people—that other children might be adopted as a result and that all the proceeds from *The Waiting Child* would be designated for a foundation to help the orphans who remained in China. Six-year-old Jaclyn did not need to be convinced. "You tell the other mamas," she told me emphatically.

When I gathered all the e-mails I had written about her—relying on the archives of friends who had saved them—I had more than 600,000 words. The book that followed was 120,000 words. I had no idea what I was doing. No experience, no skills, no agent, no publisher. All I had was a story and the naïveté of a person who has absolutely no idea how hard it is to publish a book. If I'd had a clue about what a long shot the whole thing was, I would never have started it.

An unknown writer with no credentials sent a collection of e-mails out cold to literary agents. Amazingly, two experienced agents vied for the chance to represent that work. Later, two prominent publishers competed for the rights to publish the story. In the highly competitive, tightly networked world of publishing, a small miracle had occurred: an unknown writer was actually published.

Then I discovered that writing and publishing a book is a snap compared to promoting it. Jaclyn stepped up to the challenge. At the age of seven she dutifully, with nary a complaint, signed thousands of books, often doing so in her pajamas before school started.

She gave me her non-negotiable boundaries regarding speaking engagements—she could not bear to be in the room when I spoke and hear her story told again. She would not, under any circumstances, watch the film clip, stealthily recorded, of her heart-wrenching goodbye to the child she had mothered when she left the orphanage.

Because she knew all the proceeds were designated for a charity benefiting the orphans still in China, she narrowed her eyes suspiciously at anyone she suspected might be short-changing her. She tolerated waving to audiences and having her picture taken. Then the real reward came. Within a year of the book's publication, she was able to meet—on multiple occasions—children who had been adopted because someone's heart was changed by her story. These little ones flew into her arms as if they knew her.

They followed her like she was a pied piper. One special little girl was even named after her.

At least one of us was brave. I started my book tour in the NBC studios in New York. As I waited for hours in the green room, I begged God not to let me throw up from nervousness on national TV. At my first big speaking engagement, I wore a long skirt so my shaky knees could not be seen by the audience. Right before I spoke, the national anthem was sung, and I forgot every single word. But none of that compared to the fear I felt at a mega-church in Ohio, when I faced the daunting challenge of speaking to more than two thousand people, having to remember all the technical cues and to stand on the designated mark on the stage, and still remember what I was supposed to say.

Cindy and Jaclyn with John Walsh
at NBC studios in New York

I survived it all with one simple strategy. I asked God, over and over, to just use me and let His words flow through me. And He has. When I confessed this to a friend in the audience once, she told me, "I believe that. Because as I watched you up there on the TV screen, I didn't even recognize you. It was like you were a different person."

God has a great sense of humor. He gave a story that had to be told to a woman who had never taken a writing class. He took the most directionally-impaired lady in America to more than fifty appearances all over the US. And He gave her a voice so she could speak for those who have no voice.

I think there's a method to this madness. By rising so far above what we are capable of doing ourselves, by reaching for possibilities that are so far beyond our expectations, we enable others to reflect on their possibilities too. My dear friend Deb confirmed this for me by admitting, "When my husband and I decided to adopt internationally, I looked at you—a person who still lives ten minutes from the house she grew up in, who has never really traveled, who always looks for shortcuts around the hard stuff— and figured if you could do it, it couldn't be *that* hard."

Jesus didn't pick the most competent people—religious leaders or rabbis—to be His disciples. He chose regular folks with good hearts who clearly didn't have a clue what they were getting themselves into. In fact, most of the characters in the Bible were pretty screwed up. They made mistakes, failed, lost their way—but with a mixture of faith and forgiveness, they went on to find the path God had chosen for them. They were a messed-up bunch. They were a lot like us.

We don't always choose our path in life; sometimes the path chooses us. But with God's leading, even the least capable of us can achieve things we couldn't have imagined in a million years.

Our path can lead others to greater possibilities.

Maybe the most important thing to remember about finding our way is that all of our paths are intertwined; none of us walks alone. I found my greatest purpose in life when my path intersected with that of a four-year-old orphan. But the road to her adoption began years before that.

After seeing documentaries on TV about the plight of Chinese orphans, I tried to forget them. I tried and tried. Every night on the news we learn about so many tragic stories of the plights of people all over the world. It's overwhelming to contemplate the day-to-day suffering that is commonplace in every corner of the world. It's easier to just block it all out.

But for some reason the sound of those orphaned babies crying echoed in my heart. I began to research the situation in China through the miracle of this new tool called "the web." I looked for an organization I could donate to, hoping to ease my conscience. Slowly, over time, the idea that I could be some small part of the solution began to take shape. But even if I was willing to adopt a child, how could I find out how to do it?

At that time, international adoption hadn't really taken hold in the US. I didn't know anyone who had adopted, not even domestically. I didn't even know anyone who was adopted. I had no idea how to choose an adoption agency, what the regulations were, what would be required of us. If this was the path I was meant to travel, I needed someone to guide me.

I told my mother about my interest in adopting from China. A few weeks later, she was out in her yard gardening. She noticed out

of the corner of her eye a new mother proudly pushing a baby carriage. Inside that carriage was a beautiful baby girl with shining black
hair and almond-shaped eyes. My mother hurried over to introduce
herself to this stranger and to ooh and aah over her baby. Then she
told this mom that her daughter was interested in adopting from
China and asked if she would be willing to help.

That chance encounter led to the contact I needed to guide me
toward the path that was my destiny. And that first adoption led to a
second. Then my best friend adopted two children from China. And
then her sister. And my sister. And her sister-in-law. And my cousin.
And my mom's college roommate's son. And on and on it went. Like
a stone thrown into a pond makes bigger and bigger ripples, each act
of love inspired another.

When we step out in love, we have no idea who is watching us.
We don't know who might be inspired to search their own hearts.
Who may be moved toward action. Who will be willing to step out.
Our journey can inspire someone else to take that first step. Our
path can lead others to greater possibilities. *But first we have to
step out.*

The mistake we make is in seeing our choices as limited and our
path as narrow. But possibilities abound. And even the most convoluted path can lead you to your destiny.

This is not to suggest that our path in life is always easy. We
stumble. We fail. We fall down. But we can rise again, secure in the
knowledge that every footstep brings us closer to the place where we
were meant to be. Life is full of choices. Life is full of paths. Seize
the gift of those possibilities.

The Eighth Gift

Purpose

*W*e live in a time when our children are told that if they work hard and dream big, they can be anything that they want to be. Here's the reality check: it's a big lie. And it's a big lie that isn't serving anyone well. We can't all be surgeons, no matter how much we may want to. We can't all be opera stars, no matter how much we practice. We can't all be gardeners, even if our hearts are in it. (I have the pots of wilted flowers as proof.)

The truth is simple. We all have our own special gifts and talents. They are as different as the patterns in snowflakes. And we all have our unique purpose as well—the thing we are called to do with our lives to make it matter that we lived. Our place in this world is where we fit our piece into the puzzle of life. And just like we can't force a jigsaw piece to fit in the wrong space, we have no peace when we don't follow our divine purpose. Our purposes are different, but no one's is better or worse, greater or lesser. All the notes are required to make a beautiful chorus.

The biggest struggle for most people is to figure out that purpose that is uniquely theirs. Many make the mistake of looking at movie and television stars as models. We want to be visible. We want to be on stage, not back on the prop crew. We seek our destiny in greatness—which is narrowly defined as linked to fame or money or status.

The simplest way to find your purpose in life is this: inventory your gifts, talents, and abilities. The place where your talent intersects with your determination is where your purpose lies. And generally, that place is right in front of our noses. Our purpose may be the child we are blessed to nurture, the partner we were born to love, the kindness we were put into this world at this precise moment to offer, the compliment that made someone's day . . . the accumulation of a lifetime of caring.

Purpose defines our work. Purpose defines our choices. Purpose defines our love. A life without purpose is simply wasted. But for those who choose to live purposefully, this focus becomes the defining gift of life.

Seek ovations of the heart.

On a cold Friday afternoon near the end of October, I headed off to the airport after a long, stress-filled week at work. It was the last place I wanted to go. All I wanted to do was drive home, hunker down in my house, have a hot dinner and a warm bath, and go to bed early. And I deserved it. I worked in a busy human resources department at a community college. We were in the midst of contract negotiations while simultaneously trying to mull through hundreds of job applications, answer myriad questions, counsel employees, and process requests for everything from assistance with retirement applications to approving special time-off requests. By the end of the week, the pressure of giving all the politically correct answers to a variety of problems had worn me out. I needed to slide into a cocoon of silence—no phones, no appointments, no requests. But it was not to be on this day.

Months ago I had agreed to be the keynote speaker at an adoption conference in Minneapolis—one of the few spots in the country even more cold and gray than Detroit. I was scheduled to open the event, which meant I was to take the podium at eight a.m. on a Saturday morning. So much for sleeping in. I always said yes to such invitations. My soul needed to give back in some way through volunteer activities like this. But my heart wasn't in it. This appearance brought with it all the usual stress inherent in public speaking and also robbed me of a much-needed weekend break.

Adding to my self-pity were the travel logistics. My scheduled flight wouldn't arrive in Minneapolis until well after midnight. After an hour-long drive to the venue, checking in, and settling in, combined with my inherent uneasiness about sleeping in strange hotel rooms, I figured I'd get about five hours of sleep before show time. A recipe for disaster if ever there was one.

The only ray of hope was a flight that left at seven p.m. The airline had placed me on the stand-by list. If I managed to get on that flight, I could at least get a full night's rest. If I didn't, I'd be sitting around the airport for another four hours, waiting for my later flight.

I limped up to the ticket counter to confirm my stand-by status. I'd been suffering from sporadic nerve pain in my left foot, and it was throbbing. To make matters worse, I had on high-heeled boots that seemed perfect that morning, when my foot didn't hurt, but proved foolish now that my imprisoned foot ached.

The ticket agent confirmed that I was number one on the stand-by list. She told me it seemed likely I would make the flight, which she indicated was scheduled to depart from gate #7.

I hurried to security, only to be herded into a throng of people so desperate for plastic zip-lock baggies that a cunning entrepreneur with a box of them could have walked away with a pocket full of money. Just three days earlier, the Transportation Security Authority had passed the new regulation that carry-on liquids had to be smaller than three ounces and all liquid items had to fit in a quart-size baggie. None of us had gotten this memo, and now we all scrambled.

I pasted on a big smile as I put my carry-on on the conveyor, hoping my toothpaste, deodorant, and make-up would clear inspection. No chance.

I tried to make a case that my stick deodorant wasn't technically a liquid. I tried to bargain to bring just one item with me. Then I groveled. I told the security agent I was the keynote speaker for a major conference in the morning and that I wouldn't be able to find a store in a strange city to purchase these items late at night and with no car. There were no drug stores at the airport. And honestly, would you want to listen to a keynote speaker who hadn't brushed her teeth, was sweaty, and wore no make-up? My own family had rarely seen me without make-up—it was not an image I wanted to inflict on unsuspecting strangers.

This cajoling was met with an unsmiling no. My toiletries were thrown in a trash bin along with everyone else's. Great.

Hobbling on my throbbing foot, with my toiletry-free but still heavy carry-on bag, I made my way to gate #7, which of course was at the end of the concourse. Squinting at the sign, I saw that a flight to Phoenix was posted. I walked to the counter to inquire about my flight. The ticket agent looked at me like I was the village idiot and said that my flight was at gate #77. At the opposite end of the terminal. Swell.

My foot throbbed so painfully I could hardly put any pressure on it. I found a magazine stand and bought a bottle of eight ibuprofen pills for five dollars. I limped to the closest drinking fountain and swallowed four. They did nothing to diminish my pain.

By the time I made it to gate #77, I had to clench my teeth to keep from screaming out in agony. I slumped in the chair closest to the ticket counter so I could jump up quickly if I was lucky enough to get the stand-by spot. The thought of sitting there for four more hours to catch the next flight was beyond my threshold of endurance.

As I sat there, I took inventory of my miseries. I was exhausted, cranky, and in excruciating pain. I was giving up my precious weekend. I was supposed to speak publicly—something I dreaded. Worse, I'd be facing a group of strangers with an unmasked face and sweaty armpits. Disaster.

And then I heard it. It was the unmistakable sound of a sniffle.

I glanced to my left and saw a woman about my age sitting three chairs away from me. Tears flowed freely down her face, but she seemed oblivious to them. Everyone around her averted their gaze. The man next to her lifted his newspaper higher to block the sight of her grief-stained face. The woman across from her looked down and studied her shoes. A young man increased the volume on his iPod. I looked away too. I kept waiting for someone to do something. Someone who wasn't me.

After several minutes, I couldn't stand it any longer. I moved to the empty chair next to her, leaned in, and quietly asked the stupid question that we always ask when it is patently clear that things are not okay, "Are you okay?"

She stared blankly into space for a moment, and then looked at me as if I was just coming into focus. She nodded.

Good. I was free to move back now. I had done my duty.

But something made me stay.

I patted her arm and told her I'd listen if she wanted to talk. She didn't. We sat there in silence for several minutes. Then the flood gates opened. In a rush of words, one tumbling over the next, she told me she had just gotten a call saying that her mom was dying. She wanted desperately to get to Minneapolis in time to say goodbye. She was number six on the stand-by list, and the airline personnel had told her there was little chance she would get on this flight.

Oh. I'd like to say that I immediately offered to give her my number-one spot. I'd like to say that I was gracious about doing it. I'd like to say it, but it wouldn't be true. I listened and nodded and put my arm around her shoulders. And I wrestled with my conscience big time.

My foot really hurt. I had an important event in the morning. I had to get some rest. People who'd paid money to attend this conference were counting on me to be at my best. I had already been waiting hours for that stand-by spot. As all the excuses to justify my selfish choice piled up, I knew I had no choice.

I asked her name. Then I walked to the podium before I had time to reconsider. I told the lady I had already bugged four times about my place on the list to switch my name with hers.

I went back to the grieving woman and told her she was now number one on the stand-by list. She tried to thank me, but I brushed her gratitude away. Even I knew it was the least any decent person would do.

She began to talk to me about her mother. As memories spilled out, I listened closely. And I thought with a pang, *I am so lucky. My mom is still alive.* I thought of all my petty complaints and realized that none of that mattered because I still had my mom.

We sat there, clasping hands, bound by her need for comfort and my need to offer comfort. Then a new problem arose. Where would she go when she got to Minneapolis? How would she get from the airport to the hospital? Though I consider myself the most directionally impaired person in the US, I was familiar with the Minneapolis airport. I wrote down specific instructions for her. I also told her that if I managed to get on the plane, I'd find her as soon as we got off and make sure she found her way.

Amazingly, I did get on that flight. In the way that karma seems to pay us back with interest, at the last minute one of the airline personnel walked up to me and offered me an unclaimed seat—in first class.

I found my new friend as soon as she deplaned in Minneapolis. She clung to me as if I were her lifeline as I shepherded her downstairs to a waiting cab. When we parted, she gave me a bigger hug than anyone had given me in a long, long time.

The next morning, after my speech, I got a standing ovation. And I realized in that moment that the applause of the crowd was in no way connected to my purpose in being there. I was brought to that place, under just those circumstances, because the woman in the airport needed someone. And I was that someone.

The only way to change the future is to invest in a child.

I was fortunate enough early in my career to be in the right place at the right time with the right skills. As a result, I found myself in an executive-level position while still in my twenties. I was proud of the work my employer did and threw myself headlong into proving myself worthy of this position. I literally worked day and night—often at work until eleven p.m. I was single and childless, and this job became my life. I gave it my talents, my energy, my tenacity, and even my heart.

Years later, with great angst, I resigned from this position after the birth of my first child. I walked away from ten years of outstanding commitment. And, much to my chagrin, the new guy changed pretty much everything I had done. I was virtually forgotten within weeks.

Through this experience, I learned an important life lesson: work is work. It's a means to an end. If you invest yourself in bricks and mortar and profit and see your value reflected in your paycheck, you will leave very little of lasting significance behind.

There are exceptions. Some are lucky enough or wise enough to choose careers that link perfectly with their life's purpose. Teachers are at the top of that list. And Mrs. Adams is at the top of my list.

By the time she was six, Christy could read. For most children, this is nothing extraordinary. But this little girl began her life in a Chinese orphanage, without the nutrition or sensory stimulation a growing brain and body need to properly develop. Without heat, without medical care, without love or hope. She languished in her crib, swaddled so she could hardly move, lying in her own waste until her bottom became scarred. She came to me at six months of age, lacking even the muscle tone necessary to lift her head. To make matters worse, she was saddled with a mom too ignorant to recognize Failure to Thrive Syndrome and who, as a result, did not get her the early intervention she so desperately needed.

By the time Mrs. Adams met her, Christy had already been in three different schools, and each experience had been a failure. When I had gone to observe her class at Montessori school, all the other children had been busy working on lessons; my daughter was lying on a bookcase. After I pointed this out to the teacher, she told me, "Every child is working to the best of their ability."

By the time Christy entered her third school, she had learned her own way of coping. When she anticipated that the day's lesson was beyond her ability, she told the teacher she was tired, curled up in a corner, and slept until the activity was over. As her confidence eroded, her shyness increased, and she found it nearly impossible to make friends. Every time I heard her tentatively ask, "Am I smart?" my heart broke a little bit more.

Then she met Mrs. Adams. Under her tutelage and loving guidance, Christy changed almost immediately. Within six weeks, the child who'd regularly begged me for "hooky days" could hardly wait to get to school in the morning. Sometimes she groaned when I picked her up at the end of the day, because she wanted to stay.

One afternoon she greeted me jubilantly with a paper clutched in her hand, saying, "Mrs. Adams says you're going to fall off your chair when you see what I did today!"

As her confidence grew, so did her circle of friends. She had to hug several little buddies before we could go home. One morning as we walked into the building, I asked her, "Do you know why Mommy loves you so much?" Her answer, when it came, literally stopped me in my tracks: "Because I'm smart!"

To be a great teacher is a gift. Few have it, but those who do have the capacity for change beyond the reach of others. I stand in awe of these special few, because most of us never get a chance to make a real difference, a lasting difference with our lives. But for one little girl, Mrs. Adams made all the difference.

Christy and Mrs. Adams, her remarkable teacher

There is no such thing as "just a mom."

If a friend can be a soul mate, I found that in Holly. I could call her in the middle of any crisis, and she'd know just what to say to me to make it better. I could confess to her my biggest screwups, my darkest moments, my secret fears, and she still loved me. She could also help me laugh about them, which, most of the time, was exactly the perspective I needed. Remarkable friends, the ones who understand us and still manage to love us, are one of the greatest blessings in life.

The unique thing about my friendship with Holly is that I have only been with her in person three times. She lives in Arizona; I live in Michigan. We met through such a series of unlikely coincidences, in China of all places, that I knew God had brought into my life the exact person I needed at that moment.

Holly is one of the bravest people I know. Before I met her, she was the mother of four wonderful, well-adjusted, happy children. She had a comfortable life as a suburban mom married to a successful business owner. She taught sign language at the local college. She had it all. But she felt restlessness in her soul, believing there was more that she was meant to do. This led her on a ten-year journey that included the international adoption of a deaf and emotionally impaired six-year-old named Sam, the rescue and adoption of a feisty four-year-old girl from the ravages of a war-torn country, and the adoption of an eleven-year-old named Juan with a host of medical problems and uncertain diagnoses.

On the verge of the trip to bring Juan home, Holly had a moment of panic. She reached out to me through e-mail, just as I had to her on many occasions. Our messages to each other were often several pages long and convoluted, written in the dark hours of night when fear seems to wreak havoc on good intentions. Both of us knew that at the receiving end of our e-mail was the one person who could tamp down the fear that plagues even the most determined mothers. We didn't dismiss each other's fears with false assurances. Fear is real, and international adoption is not without scary risks—for the moms who choose to love the child of another and also for their families. I considered her fears and wrote back, as honestly as I could, how I saw the balance between the "what ifs" in her choice.

What if Juan has medical problems well beyond those you know about?

What if Juan needs more than one surgery?

What if he has adjustment issues beyond just being a scared eleven-year-old boy on the other side of the earth, far from everything familiar?

What if Juan acts out and causes more chaos in your life?

What if he will never be physically normal?

What if Juan has serious emotional issues related to his life of pain and rejection?

What if he can't get along with Sam?

On the other hand . . .

What if Juan blesses your life with a spirit of kindness?

What if he connects with Sam and is able to touch that part of him that you can't touch—that part that is still a frightened boy whose world was turned upside down?

What if Juan teaches, by example, what it means to accept your limitations?

What if he models gratefulness?

What if he inspires just one more person to adopt an older child?

What if Juan graduates from college and becomes a teacher and touches the lives of countless other kids?

What if he grows up to become a volunteer for Habitat for Humanity and brings joy to homeless families?

What if he becomes a loving husband and father and gives you wonderful grandchildren to love in your old age?

What if Juan teaches you something about life and the preciousness of it that you don't know now?

What if he grows up and adopts too, and one of his children fulfills a divine purpose?

I reminded her that God would not forsake her. He brought these kids to her for a reason; their lives have purpose beyond what we can fathom. I assured her that if she didn't dance with fear she wouldn't be normal, because changing your life to make room for another is scary beyond words. Just like everything else worth doing.

A few years later I found out that Holly had expanded her family further to include foster children. Yet her spirit was restless to do even more, just as mine was. We shared the common experience of being in third-world-country orphanages and staring into the eyes of want. Nothing in life looks the same after that. We both wanted to do more. We needed to do more. But the boundaries of our current lives—the families who needed us, the work that paid the bills—kept us stuck firmly in place.

I confessed to her the growing dissatisfaction I had with a life that seemed ordinary in a world with extraordinary needs. Was it ever enough to be "just a mom"?

Holly understood this longing in my heart. She responded, "If I could hop on a plane tomorrow and go back to Mother Theresa's Orphanage and Home for the Dying, I would." I felt the same way. Holding dying babies who were feverish and underweight was engraved on our minds forever.

Holly remembered one such little one had the softest, weakest whimper she'd ever heard. He only stopped when she nuzzled him in her neck and sang softly to him. Putting him back in a crib and walking away was one of the hardest things she had ever done. The guilt that we could not do more was immense, but what could we do? Smuggle children out of their country?

At least he was a fighter, although for how much longer I could not know. The ones who didn't respond at all when someone picked them up or talked to them were even more heartbreaking. They did not have much longer in this world.

These are children of God, with the same value our own children have, but they are too far removed from our lives to seem real to most of us.

"When my kids are grown and gone," Holly told me, "my dream is to go to Haiti or China or Africa or wherever the Lord leads me and just rock babies."

What Holly understood was that there is a real difference between doing what we are called to do and doing work that impresses others.

Since we are taught that our value is measured in dollars and recognition, no one is impressed by what mothers do, working 24/7 with endless demands, middle-of-the-night crises, dirty diapers, and whining toddlers. If being a mom was a paying job, no one would take it. Love is what makes it worthwhile. Love makes motherhood tolerable on days when you are trapped inside by dreary rain and think that if you have to sweep up spilled Cheerios one more time, you will lose it.

Being a good mom makes a difference in the world, even if the impact seems small in the grand scheme of things. After all, even the guy who landed on the moon was once a scared little boy who needed his mom.

Maybe the work you were intended to do at this time in your life is not serving the poor in a third-world country, but tending the garden in front of you. Protecting the tender shoots. Plucking out the thorns of hurtful words and deeds before they damage your precious children. Weeding out intolerance, disrespect, and cynicism. Watering your young sprouts with love and kindness. And praying for a good harvest.

The ultimate measure of our success is the kindnesses we leave behind.

Shortly after the start of the new year, I got a late-night call from my best friend, Deb. Her dear father had suffered a massive stroke and died. My heart ached for her and her family. Later, when funeral arrangements were being made, I asked if I could have the honor of sharing a story about her dad at the service.

I arrived at the funeral home early. The large main room was packed; all the overflow rooms combined could not contain the mourners. When the minister asked if anyone wanted to say a few words, I made my way to the front and shared my story.

During my freshman year in college, I became good friends with Deb, my suite mate. I sat with her one evening and flipped through her photo album from home. I asked her about a picture of a large oak tree with a big hand-painted wooden sign hanging on it that read "That's my girl!" Deb explained that when she graduated from high school, she was valedictorian of her class. Her dad wanted to make sure everyone in their small town knew of his joy. So he went to the barn and grabbed a big sheet of ply-wood and painted a sign to hang from a tree in the front yard so there could be no mistaking his pride.

The picture of that memorial to love touched my heart. I wondered what it felt like to be loved that much.

I soon found out that to know Deb was to know her fam-ily. I enjoyed getting to know both her dad and her mom. They embraced me early on, saying that if I was Deb's friend, I was welcome any time. They made sure I knew I always had an open invitation to visit their home.

Over the years, their support was always there. The first year after my divorce, they called me before the holidays to see how I was doing and make sure I knew I was welcome at their table. When I had speaking engagements, I often saw their faces in the audience. They appeared at an evening adoption support group I facilitated—I suspect to fill the seats in case no one showed up. I teasingly called them my "groupies." Their love was visible.

Because this family had been changed by adoption, just as mine had, they knew that family is defined by love, not by blood. Deb's parents proudly gave me an "adoption certificate" they had created to indicate that I was considered a full-fledged member of their clan. I framed it and displayed it on my mantel.

There is a long-standing tradition in publishing that when a new book is released, the editor of that book plucks the first copy off the press and presents it, often with a nice note or inscription, to the author. When my first book was released, the publisher was in New York and I was in Michigan. That first ceremonial copy arrived by FedEx on a cold Tuesday night. When I opened the package, I looked with teary eyes at the culmination of so much work. I wanted to share that moment with someone who would understand my joy, so I called the person who was closer to me than a sister: Deb. Even though it was a school night and she had three young daughters and homework and dinner and baths and errands and lived forty minutes away, she piled her family into the car to come celebrate that moment with me. We talked and laughed and hugged and turned the pages of the long-awaited book.

A little after nine that evening, my doorbell rang. I couldn't imagine who would be visiting at that hour. There, on my front porch, stood Deb's parents. They had made a two-hour drive on that bitter cold night to be with me. Deb's dad held a big wooden handmade sign to hang from the tree in my front yard. It read "That's my girl!"

When I finished telling my story at that funeral service, before I could take my seat, Deb's brother grabbed my hand and thanked me for sharing a story he had never heard. Then he whispered, "When I think of my three Chinese nieces who would not be here if it hadn't been for your influence on our family, I imagine God looking down at you, smiling, and saying, 'That's *my* girl.'"

With tears in my eyes, I tried to make my way to my seat. It was difficult to move through the throng of people who were lined up to tell their own stories about Deb's dad.

One woman spoke of how Deb's parents had stayed up with her all night praying after her husband had life-threatening surgery.

Another man stood up and said that he, too, had been invited to join this family. He had been a lost twelve-year-old when his dad left the family in dire economic straits. Deb's father stepped up to become his fill-in dad.

Another friend told of visiting him on the day he died and hearing him determinedly trying to share his faith with the doctor taking his medical history. A woman spoke of his warm smile and encouraging words to her at a dark point in her life.

Perhaps the most compelling story came from a man who said that Deb's dad had visited every week while he was in prison, never allowing him to give up hope. Every week for forty years.

Deb's mom and dad with their special sign

After more than two hours of these stories, with no end in sight, the minister finally called an end to the service.

Deb's brother finished with these final remarks: "Because my dad had so many friends, on the day he died he had three ministers come to see him. The hospital staff must have thought he was a really holy man. Or a despicable sinner who desperately needed help." The crowd chuckled. "My dad was neither of these. He was a simple man who loved God and wanted to share that love with others. He simply chose every day to love."

A few weeks later, a man I knew professionally died. I secretly disliked him, but my position required me to make an appearance at his funeral. He had used the power and authority of his role to control and berate others. He laughed once when he told me about an employee crying after he had dressed her down. He was a tough taskmaster who confused fear with respect.

He had several graduate degrees. He'd had great career success. He had traveled everywhere. He'd been powerful and had rubbed shoulders with many influential leaders. He left behind a huge pile of money.

I was one of eight people at his funeral.

As I stood there, watching the tearless faces of pseudo-mourners, I thought of the contrast between these two funerals.

Deb's dad wasn't educated. He'd driven a truck for a local bakery. He had never traveled more than a few hours from his small town. He'd never met anyone famous or influential. His bank account was puny.

What he left behind was a big pile of kindnesses. And isn't that the true measure of a life?

Be the one who applauds.

One Sunday as I drove to church, the girls, who were six, eight, and ten, looked out the car window and noticed dozens of women of all ages and sizes striding purposefully down the sidewalk on a three-day, sixty-mile breast cancer Walk for the Cure.

"What are all those ladies doing, Mama?" Jaclyn asked.

I blanched at how to explain this horrific disease to my children. But I did. I told them how special these walkers were because they were showing how much they cared about fighting a terrible illness. I told them about my cousin who had died of this disease. I told them that many of these walkers might have had breast cancer themselves, or had someone they loved afflicted by it. I told them how far sixty miles was. I wasn't sure how much they understood.

As we approached the stoplight, the girls rolled down the car windows and exuberantly applauded. I felt foolish for not having thought to do the same. After all, if we're not in the game, shouldn't we at least be on the sidelines cheering? And what could be more important than celebrating the triumph of compassion over complacency?

That night at bedtime, Jaclyn told God, "Thank You for the ladies who walk so far to help the sick people." A few days later she asked me what those ladies were called. Stumped for an answer, I said, "Volunteers?"

"How do you spell that?" Jaclyn asked. I spelled the word for her.

A few days later, I found a book she had made out of construction paper. The front cover said, "Jaclyn's Jobs for When She Grow Up and Moves to Florida." On the inside page, she'd written:

1. Cheerleader
2. Lifeguard
3. Mickey Mouse helper
4. Volunteer

We never know who is watching our example. We never know who will take up the banner next.

Compassion is contagious.

Our greatest triumphs are revealed in our smallest acts of love.

I first heard about Jaclyn's birth mother six weeks after I adopted her. Jaclyn came to me before I was out of bed one morning and said matter-of-factly, "Jack-win have two mamas."

I was stunned. Until that moment, it hadn't occurred to me that a child abandoned as a toddler would remember her birth mom. I waited to hear what would come next.

"One go-away Chinese mama," she said, not allowing herself to feel the sting of that designation. "One this-a mama," she said, pointing at me.

I nodded "yes," happy in the comparative scheme of things with this designation.

Jaclyn paused, carefully choosing her next words. "I no want go-away Chinese mama. I want this-a mama."

With a great sigh of relief, I said, "I'm so glad! Because I want you too."

Then she revealed her heart. "Jack-win scared."

"What are you afraid of?"

"I scared this-a mama go away." Her eyes locked on mine.

I quickly assured her that I would never go away. That she would be my child always.

She listened to my words carefully but weighed them against her life experience. Why, after all, should she trust me when so many others had let her down?

Being the pragmatic child she was, Jaclyn made her own Plan B. A few days later, I noticed her small Mickey Mouse suitcase at the end of her bed. I peeked inside and saw a stash of her favorite things—a red sequined purse, sparkly tights that she loved, her plastic Barbie dishes. I knew why the suitcase was there, but I still asked anyway.

"In case I have to go in a hurry, I want to have all my best and most favorite things," she replied. I again offered assurances. But the suitcase remained in place—a daily reminder of the failures of those who should have loved her most.

Understanding that her security was tenuous, I repeated a mantra every time I went anywhere. "Mama goes. But mama always comes back. Mama will always come back for Jaclyn." She heard those words every time I left her, even if it was just to take out the trash. But hearing the words and believing them were two different things.

A few months later, there was a distinct moment that revealed our evolving relationship. Because she had helped care for toddlers in the orphanage, Jaclyn's mothering instincts often spilled over into concern for her little sister. Because Christy was notoriously shy, getting her to stay at Sunday school without hysterical tears was a struggle. I had almost given up.

One week, Christy asked her big sister, "You stay with me, Gockwin?" When Jaclyn nodded, she decided to stay at Sunday school.

Afterward, I asked Jaclyn how it had gone.

"She cry for a little while," Jaclyn reported. "She want her mama." Then she added, "She not know you always come back."

Jaclyn's understanding amazed me. I asked, "Do you know that I will always come back for you?"

She nodded. "You no be go-away mama. You be always-come-back mama!"

And it was evident, finally, that she believed this in her soul. What a long way we had come in less than a year.

Then she added, "I no be go-away baby. I be always-come-back baby. I *always be your baby.*"

I hadn't thought of our covenant as being two-sided. But I felt reassured by her promise. Because if she ever went away, it would be like the sun had stopped shining in my life.

Later that week I noticed the suitcase had moved from the end of her bed to the closet.

And then it was gone.

I have had a few triumphs in my life. Forgive me for boring you with them, but I was high school valedictorian in a class of more than six hundred students. I had my first executive-level job when I was twenty-seven. I published a book with a prestigious New York publisher, and I've been interviewed on national television. But all of that pales in comparison to my greatest triumph—gaining the trust of that precious child on the day the suitcase disappeared.

~~~~

There is no intersection between logic and purpose. Sometimes our purpose makes no logical sense, but we know in our hearts it is what God is asking us to do, the thing that will define us. And the reward associated with it rarely comes in the form of a paycheck.

Our life's purpose is found in our connection to one another. When we are there for others, we serve our highest purpose.

How do we know when our purpose is fulfilled? If you're still drawing breath, you're not done yet. As long as we live, we have the power within us to love.

When I think back on my life, the moments that stand out—the memories that are in vivid color in an otherwise black-and-white movie—are those times when I reached beyond myself and risked something to love someone. Those are the moments when I found my purpose.

We are all here for a reason. There are no unplanned births. The circumstances surrounding a conception may be accidental, but our lives are intentional. God delivers no mistakes.

When you focus on purpose, the junk in your life falls away. Purpose fuels your heart. And for this reason, it is an amazing gift of life.

Powerful Truths

The things we know for sure are our truths, and they become the guiding force in our lives. One of the gifts in living, suffering, experiencing, growing, and changing is having those truths revealed to us. What we once believed to be true often changes. What we want to be true sometimes proves false. But if we live without honoring our truths, our lives will be full of turmoil. The only way to live in peace is to know our own truths. And to live them.

Compassion requires action.

Part of the joy of being a new parent is experiencing your child's firsts. His or her first words. First steps. The first tooth.

When my oldest, Kate, was two, she excitedly anticipated her first movie in a real theatre. We had no problem selecting the film—it had to be Disney's latest cartoon release, *The Hunchback of Notre Dame*.

Kate had received a stuffed Quasimodo for her second birthday and immediately fell in love. She dubbed him Fazzy-moto, and he became her continual companion. One night I had to sneak him out of her arms while she slept so I could give him a much-needed spin in the washing machine. Unfortunately, that first washing resulted in his red hair turning into a big fuzz ball. With trepidation, I slipped him back into Kate's arms. When she

Kate and her beloved Fazzy-moto

awoke, she looked at him, puzzled by his overnight change in appearance. Then she reassured him. "Don't worry, Fazzy. It's just a bad hair day."

Her father often played ventriloquist with him, making him speak back to her in a hysterically gravelly voice, which added to his charm.

Kate started to ask me once if he was real and then stopped herself. Of course he was real.

It was a given that Fazzy would accompany us to her first movie experience. After all, he was the star of the show. The three of us piled into the car on a cold, sunny Saturday and drove to our local theatre. It was the perfect venue for an outing of this magnitude—a historic relic with vaulted, gilded ceilings and heavy velvet drapes. I told Kate that because this was a special day, she could have any treat she wanted from the concession stand. She settled on M&Ms, popcorn, and a Coke.

I grabbed a plastic booster chair, and we found great seats—close to the front and in the dead center of the row. Kate settled Fazzy in next to her, then hunkered down in her booster chair, treats beside her, joyfully expectant of the film to come.

Within the first ten minutes of the movie, a brutal scene unfolded on the screen—Quasimodo was ridiculed by the townsfolk while strapped to a giant wheel. Kate's eyes grew wide in horror as the mocking continued. When one of the townspeople hurled a tomato at the humiliated hunchback, Kate couldn't stand it any longer. Literally sick with compassion, she reached for the popcorn bucket and wretched in it.

I whispered in her ear, "Do you want to leave?"

She immediately said yes. Clutching Fazzy close to her and covering his eyes, she stoically walked away. Everyone else in the theater kept munching on their treats, caught up in the action, seemingly unaffected by the scene. It was, after all, just a movie. And an animated one at that.

Kate is now a senior in high school. To this day she has never been able to watch *The Hunchback of Notre Dame*. As surprised as I was that she wanted to leave that theatre so long ago, I was secretly proud of her revulsion. Cruelty should make us sick—no matter the form, no matter our age. And to sit by and passively watch? Desensitized to the suffering of others, too often we take no action.

Our feet speak. Get up. Walk out. Speak out. Reach out. I learned that the day a two-year-old taught me that compassion requires action.

They can beat you, but they can't defeat you.

As Kate grew older, she changed in nearly every way but one. The compassion in her heart seemed to grow along with her. Late in the evening one night when the girls were visiting friends, Kate called me. As soon as she heard my voice, she broke down into hysterical sobs. Something bad had happened. She had promised not to tell. But she had to tell.

I assumed her tears were for herself, but her heartache was actually for her sister Jaclyn. Between choking sobs, she conveyed that she'd been on Facebook, sending a message to her sister, when she saw other messages come in. Bullying messages from a group of teenage boys. She couldn't tell me what they said because it was "really, really bad."

I had been a teenager once myself, so I thought I knew what their "really bad" messages might be. I was also a psychologist. And a mom.

"Tell me," I urged.

But Kate couldn't bring herself to say the words. "They're too awful, Mom. They hurt too much. I can't say them."

Assuming it was sexually explicit words or profanities, I asked her if she could write them down. She agreed. Moments later, she texted the words to me on my cell phone: "No one likes you. Even your own mother didn't like you. That's why she abandoned you. You should kill yourself."

I stopped breathing, literally buckled over with pain. I fantasized about getting into my car and driving to the homes of the boys who had written those words. They had turned the knife in the most vulnerable place of any adoptee—the issue that haunts them their whole lives. How do you make sense of the fact that your mother—the one who should love you most—walked away?

I wanted to go to those boys' houses and throw them against the wall and pummel them with my fists. I wanted them to suffer for ravaging my child's heart.

Instead I fell to my knees on my kitchen floor, buried in sobs. I wanted my mom to comfort me and make it all better. But I couldn't tell her. Kate was right: the words were too awful. They hurt too much. I couldn't say them any more than my daughter could. I wanted to crawl in a hole and die.

Then I flashed back to the first day that Jaclyn was my daughter. The shock of being removed from the orphanage and whisked off by strangers was too much for her to process. She reverted to animal-like behavior—screaming and crying in agony, too insulated in her own pain to allow me to comfort her. After hours of it, I was terrified. How would I ever be enough for her? I wanted to forget this whole thing and run back to the safety of my house.

When I confessed my fear to my husband, he put it all in perspective by saying, "If we're this terrified, think of how it must be for her."

I hurt deeply over these boys' insensitive words, but the pain Jaclyn must have felt was unimaginable. And yet, she marched back into school the next day and faced her tormentors with her head held high and her shoulders squared. She forced her mind to focus on the tasks at hand.

If only I could have faked it that well. I wanted to call in sick to work, bury myself in my pillow, and not have to face this day.

But not only did I have a full schedule at work, it was also the day I taught a psychology class on my lunch hour. With only my rage fueling me after a sleepless night, I grabbed my notes to see what the topic was for class that day and smiled wryly. "Achieving Emotional Balance in a Chaotic World." This was psychology-speak for "How to tamp down your anger so you can function in life." Beyond ironic.

I started class that day by asking my students if they'd ever shown up for church and then found out the sermon was on something they were struggling with that week. Several students nodded. I told them that was what had happened to me. I was supposed to lecture on managing anger when I had been more angry in the past twenty-four hours than I'd ever been in my life.

As I reached for my lecture notes, one student asked, "Can you tell us what happened?"

I hesitated, always concerned with blurring the line between professional distance and honest engagement. But I decided to tell them. Maybe some of them had been bullied too. Or maybe some of them had been bullies.

You could hear a pin drop as I finished. Sniffles echoed around the room. One student in the back row—a big, heavily tattooed young man with a heart of gold and keen intellect hiding behind his bravado—growled, "Give me the name of those boys, Dr. C. I'll take care of them."

The African-American man next to him said, "Ask Jaclyn if she wants her big, black uncle to show up for a visit at her school." With a smile, he added, "I know how to make bullies stop. I'm there for your girl."

I smiled at their support and the way they thought to show it. I knew about the blows they'd suffered too. The week before, I'd given them an assignment—to create a timeline and record the critical events in their lives. If the event was positive, they were to record it above the timeline. Negative events were to be charted below the line. Then they were to study those charts and identify what events had motivated them the most and why.

As I graded those papers, I gasped at the revelations.

"This is the year my dad got shot."

"This was when my best friend died of an overdose."

"This is the year my mom walked out on our family."

"This was when I went to jail."

I saw now a chance to speak the truth about their experiences as well as mine.

I told them of my worst moment as Jaclyn's mom—listening to this small child recite the list of wrongs that had been committed against her before she became my daughter. The horrific truth came out in pieces as I gained her trust. At the top of the list was the beating she had endured in the orphanage. I tried to wrap my mind around it by telling myself it was a different culture with different standards and beliefs. But the vivid picture she painted of that event burned in my mind a scene I simply couldn't erase.

Years later, when I watched Jaclyn graduate from middle school, I saw a beautiful, smart, poised young woman walk proudly across the stage, and I thought, *They can beat you, but they can't defeat you.*

"You've all been beaten by life too," I told my students. "Bad stuff happens to all of us. But defeat is inside of us. We each control our own destiny. Always remember, 'They can beat you, but they can't defeat you.'"

I reminded them that, like Jaclyn, they had not been defeated. They were all in college now and working toward goals that would help them triumph over their pasts. I heard sniffles all around the room, which told me they understood. One of my students said, "We should give ourselves a round of applause!" They broke out into prolonged clapping. It was magic.

That day, they saved me.

> ## In matters of right and wrong, there is no room for rationalization.

In the fall of 2003, my family had an opportunity to visit Washington, DC. At six, eight, and ten, the girls were the perfect ages to see firsthand how our government works. Because Jaclyn would miss a few days of school, her teacher asked her to make up her schoolwork by writing an essay about what she would do if she held the nation's highest office. Here's what she wrote:

If I Were President
By Jaclyn Champnella

If I were president I'd cancel schoolwork re-do and returns, cause it gives more work to do. I'd also cancel homework, mornings (cause mornings are awful) and also brussel sprouts.

If I were president there'd be a lot of food and a lot of doctors.

If I were president you wouldn't have wars. You wouldn't have to eat foods you didn't like or have bedtimes. You wouldn't even have loneliness.

If I were president all garbage would be trees because trees keep you alive. And a person who sometimes forgot to flush the toilet would still be allowed to be president.

And with those lofty ideals in mind, we headed out for our nation's capital. I've read somewhere that the mind has a wonderful mechanism for erasing memories of pain. This is apparently what accounts for the fact that many women go through childbirth more than once. In spite of that research, and the fact that I can still vividly recall *that* pain, I had seemed to block a different painful memory—that of what a family vacation is like.

I started out this family trip, as always, with happy visions of a Norman Rockwell-ish outing. But by the second day in the car, my husband reminded me, while glancing back at the little darlings who were driving us crazy, that in the Chevy Chase movie *National Lampoon's Vacation* they drove with Grandma strapped to the roof. I mulled over that option before remembering that Grandma was dead in that scene.

Actually, the real joy had started on the plane. Jaclyn and Kate took their seats across the aisle from me. I was so busy arranging myself, Christy, and my carry-on bag of diversions, I failed to notice that Jaclyn was standing on the seat, studying the overhead buttons. When I told her to get down, she said, "I'm looking for the button for the waitress. I want a drink!"

I told her that was not how things worked, and she would have to wait with everyone else for the flight attendant to come around with soft drinks.

"That's not true," she said emphatically. "I saw people in the front of the plane with drinks."

I tried to explain to her that they were in first class, to which she huffed, "I wish I was sitting in the front."

When the flight attendant appeared in our section, she offered Jaclyn the use of a blanket.

"Head lice!" Jaclyn shrieked at her, recoiling in horror from the proffered blanket.

"Why did you say that?" I asked, embarrassed, as the flight attendant slunk away in shock.

"What if someone with head lice used that blanket before they gave it to me?" she said with annoyance.

"Oh, please," I said with matching annoyance.

"You never know where head lice are hiding, Mama," she said with authority.

I retreated from that battle.

At least there was one thing on the plane that delighted Jaclyn. "Look, Mama, I got my very own bag to throw up in," she said, hoisting the paper bag in the air.

Once we arrived in DC, I was excited about sharing with the girls the wonderful monuments I remembered being inspired by as a child. But even armed with three detailed maps, a compass in the car, and our best attempts at navigation, we made the four-mile drive from the airport to the hotel a one-hour, anxiety-ridden excursion filled with wrong turns, maddening gridlock, and endless frustration. Of course, this gave our little darlings plenty of time to annihilate one another in the backseat.

The next morning, battle lines were drawn from the minute they got out of bed.

"It isn't polite to knock on the bathroom door when someone is going to the bathroom," Kate huffed.

"I didn't knock," Jaclyn said innocently.

"It isn't polite to *kick* the door either."

"I didn't kick the door," Jaclyn replied.

"Well, it isn't nice to *lean* against the door when someone is going to the bathroom," Kate said, with rising irritation.

"I didn't lean against the door."

"Then what did you do?" Kate screamed.

"I just touched it," Jaclyn said sweetly.

"Well, it isn't nice to *touch* the door when someone is going to the bathroom!"

Game on.

At breakfast, Kate asked Jaclyn, "Why did you put a toast crumb in my cream cheese?"

I tried to diffuse this one by pointing out that Kate was finished using the cream cheese, so no harm was done. But no transgression was slight enough to be overlooked in our family. I knew the girls would lie in wait for the moment when my head was turned so they could further torture each other.

"You scratched me," Kate shrieked when Jaclyn's hand brushed her arm as we walked to the various attractions.

"Sand blew near my eye. I might be blind!" my little drama queen yelled when the wind kicked up.

"Mom, a leaf hit me in the head," Kate shrieked, apparently convinced she had suffered irreparable brain damage.

I began my usual chant:

"Stop it."

"Stop it right now."

"I mean it!"

I repeated this endlessly until I seized on the idea of taking the three of them to a park and allowing them to have a fight to the finish. The last one standing could step over her bloody sisters and proclaim herself an only child.

Their father, upon hearing my brilliant idea, had only one thing to say to me: "Stop it!"

It was our family theme.

In spite of all the fighting, the sights were incredible, even better than I remembered. Our evening tour to see the monuments lit at night filled the girls with awe. In fact, they enjoyed it more than I dared hope.

I saved the best for last. Because George Washington was Jaclyn's favorite president, I made sure we visited Mount Vernon. It was a beautiful, warm, sunny fall day, and the view of the Potomac River from the back porch of the plantation was serene and peaceful. The tour of the estate was fascinating, filled with colorful details about the life of this remarkable leader. The girls were enthralled and took in every word.

I hardly noticed how uncharacteristically quiet Jaclyn had become. As we walked down the long pathway back to the parking lot, I asked her, "What did you think of your favorite president's home?"

"He's not my favorite president anymore," she said, kicking stones in her path.

"Why not?"

"I didn't know he had slaves," she said sadly.

I tried to explain that this was common practice in those times, and that historians had noted how compassionate he was toward them, relatively speaking.

Cindy and the girls at Mount Vernon

Jaclyn would have none of it. "If I were George Washington, I would have bought all the slaves. I would have given them food and their own blankets. Then I would have made them free!"

I tried to explain that Washington was ahead of his time in terms of understating how wrong slavery was and that his will contained a provision to free his slaves upon his death.

Jaclyn cast her eyes downward. "But why did he do it if he knew it was *wrong*?"

I had no answer for this, so I didn't even attempt one.

We walked without speaking until she said, "Mama, who was the president who ended slavery?"

I told her it was Abraham Lincoln.

"He's my favorite president now."

Never stop speaking for those who have no voice.

After Jaclyn's remarkable story was published in book form, I was invited to speak to groups all over the United States. I was excited about the prospect. How many lives would be changed? How many children might be adopted? How much money would be raised for our designated charity? I couldn't wait to do this.

That was in the beginning. For months I squeezed in talks on my lunch hours. I traveled across the country, spoke, and came back in a single day. After a while, I got really tired. And cranky. Weariness crushed the excitement I started with.

After two years of juggling out-of-town speaking engagements around my full-time job while attempting to be a wife and a mother to three small children, I was done. I was so done. I couldn't wait for it to be over.

In the spring of 2005, I had three speaking engagements left—I was counting them down. The first was a keynote address at a conference in Pasadena, California. After working all week, I raced to the airport on Friday evening, hauling a heavy carton of books to be signed at the event.

At the check-in counter, I asked the airline employee if I could borrow some tape to secure a corner on my book box. The harried woman hurled a tape roll at me but gave me nothing to cut it with. When I politely asked for something to cut the tape, she handed me a pen. As I puzzled over how to cut tape with a pen, the end of the tape stuck to the roll. The airline employee glared at me. I gave up and handed the tape back.

To my shock, the airline employee screamed at me. "How am I supposed to use this now? You didn't roll the end of the tape over!"

Everyone glanced at me as I stood there, shamed by my boorish tape behavior. Later, a guy came over to me, apparently not intimidated by being seen with the boorish tape woman, and said, "I can't believe the way that lady screamed at you!"

When I got on my four-hour flight, I discovered I had won the airline seat lottery—my seat was in the next-to-last row. The one where the seats barely recline and you can hear the toilet flush the entire flight. Oh, goodie.

As soon as I sat down, a friendly woman approached, indicating that she had the seat next to me. I got up to let her in. She immediately lifted the armrest between us so she could basically sit on top of me for the rest of this four—count them, four—hour flight. Then she told me, in great detail, all about her job as a tax preparer. Apparently I looked like a person who did not understand what a tax preparer did because no minutia was left uncovered in her description.

On the other side of the aisle sat a whining toddler. I smiled sympathetically at the parents, who were obviously expecting another bundle of joy. The pregnant mother disclosed that they'd forgotten their son's backpack of stuff to amuse him with. He had no toys, no snacks, nothing to keep him occupied.

Before our four-hour flight took off, we sat on the ground for an hour. The whole time, the dad across the aisle kept saying, "No, Tyler, you can't stand on Mommy's tummy to see out the window."

My seatmate was visibly irritated by the toddler and kept complaining to me about it. I personally found having someone crowding over on my seat crushing me much more annoying. Meanwhile, the guy behind me amused himself by kicking my seat. I periodically turned around to glare at him. The guy would stop for about seven minutes and then begin again with a new rhythm. One time I turned to glare at the exact moment when the flight attendant came out of the galley with the beverage cart. I missed a direct hit in the face by about three seconds. (That would've been a nice look for a keynote speaker.)

The turbulence was so bad the flight attendants had to sit most of the flight. The plucky toddler said, "Whee!" and "Wow!" every time the plane went up and down.

During one of the few moments the flight attendants were out of their seats, trying to frantically get caught up, my seat mate rang the overhead buzzer. When the flight attendant came over, my seat mate asked, "How big is this plane?" I couldn't imagine why she'd want to know that. Did she intend to purchase it after we landed? The irritated flight attendant tossed the safety booklet at her, clearly expecting that instructions on how to put on her seat belt would answer this ridiculous question.

I closed my eyes and feigned sleep, trying desperately not to vomit from the turbulence. Moments later my seatmate said, "I have a nosebleed!" I looked at her face but saw no blood. I asked if she wanted to get up (no). If she needed a tissue (no, she had one). Then I realized she was just offering this as a public service announcement, not a call to action.

When the flight finally ended and I got off the plane, I figured the worst was behind me. I hurried to the waiting area for the shuttle bus to the hotel, which I had prearranged and prepaid.

After a long wait, a van with "TO PASADENA" in the windshield arrived. I breathed a sigh of relief as I climbed into the middle seat. Then the driver asked, "So, how do we get there?" I was stunned. When I made the arrangements, I e-mailed directions to the hotel. How could the driver of a shuttle to Pasadena not know how to get there?

I asked my four fellow passengers if any of them were from Pasadena. They appeared equally panicked. I nicely suggested to shuttle man that he call for directions, but he feigned deafness.

Driving aimlessly in heavy traffic, the driver began a bizarre recitation that sounded like cursing in a foreign language. The helpful man next to me yelled, "What are you saying?" No response. He tapped the shuttle driver on the shoulder and repeated the question more loudly. Still no response.

Finally, shuttle man pulled off the expressway and drove down a dead-end street that led to the LA library. No one on the shuttle was staying at the library, although I did contemplate getting out of the van and just sleeping in a chair there.

The driver confessed that he had no idea where to go. Helpful man suggested he call someone. Or look at a map. These were all rejected. Instead, the driver stared ahead as if waiting for divine inspiration.

Then, without warning, we were on the move again. At a stoplight, a car pulled alongside us, and the woman in the driver's seat asked for directions. Shuttle man yelled out the window, "I'm lost too!" Great.

Helpful man kept fidgeting and checking his watch. "I have to give a lecture in forty-five minutes."

A guy behind me put his face on the seat next to me and became my personal tour guide. "This is the route of the Tournament of Roses parade." (Like I missed that twelve-foot billboard announcing it.) "Do you know what the Rose Parade is?" (Does any adult in America *not* know what the Rose Parade is?) He told me about his favorite places to go in Pasadena. (Funny how he knew all these places but was no help with directions.)

He asked me what hotel I was staying at. When I gave him the name, he said he knew a good Mexican restaurant near there. He asked if I'd like to be his guest for a nice taco dinner. I like tacos about as much as I liked this guy. I politely declined, explaining that I was married. He leaned back in his seat and sulked. An uncomfortable silence descended on the van.

When we pulled up at a hotel, I asked the driver if he was sure this was the right one. Pickup guy yelled at me, "Lady, if it isn't the right one, why don't you just get a cab?" Yes, I was clearly the problem.

Apparently this was the only hotel in America that didn't have helpful people to handle guests' luggage. I dragged my suitcase across a cobblestone drive. (Who would put cobblestones in an area where people have to wheel luggage?) I got inside, exhausted, went to the check-in counter, and was told, "We don't have a reservation in your name."

Could travel get any worse?

After returning from this memorable trip to Pasadena, I spent two exhausting days at work, then headed out again—this time on a four-hour car trip to an evening speaking engagement to honor the Woman of the Year in Alpena, Michigan. I only had one more speaking engagement after this one. I couldn't wait for it all to be over.

Miraculously, I didn't get lost on the trip. I even checked into the hotel in time to freshen up. As I got out of the shower, I realized that in my haste to repack the suitcase I took to Pasadena (which never left my foyer), I had forgotten to pack clean underwear.

As I reluctantly put back on my non-fresh underwear, the hotel room phone rang. The organizer of the event, Pam, nervously asked where I was. She insisted I get to the hall immediately for the technical check. A glance in the mirror revealed that the part in my hair was really messed up. And I had forgotten to bring a comb. I grabbed a golf pencil from the hotel desk drawer and attempted to fix my hair without drawing on my head.

Wearing dirty underwear and with my hair styled by a golf pencil, I entered the convention hall. Struggling in high heels and a white suit with fifty-pound boxes of books to sell, I thought of how glamorous it *wasn't* to be a writer.

After the technical check, I made nice at the cocktail party, trying to act like the role I'd been assigned (author? speaker? entertainer?) instead of a lady who wears dirty underwear and styles her hair with a golf pencil.

I was honored to have the winner of the Woman of the Year award seated next to me. I'd been told it was to be a surprise announcement, and I was not to give it away. I had also learned that this woman, Miriam, was eighty-five years old and had spent her whole life in service to others through an impressive list of charitable activities.

Miriam sat down, and we began to chat. Struck by her incredible beauty, I asked her for the secret of her remarkable skin. She leaned over and confided, "I stopped having sex when I was forty-two." Now, there's a beauty secret I'd never heard before! I began to choke, praying that coffee would not come spewing out of my nose, as one of my goals when I spoke anywhere was to make it through the event with nothing coming out of my nose. Miriam sized up my wrinkly face with a withering glance, as if to say, *Better stop now. It's almost too late.*

I wanted to explain to her that I was usually not so wrinkly, that I hadn't been sleeping well and also had jet lag. But before I could get the words out, Miriam asked, "Are you in 'the change,' dear?" She then described, in great detail, her own experience with menopause.

No one was more excited (i.e., relieved) than I when my new friend was announced as Woman of the Year. In her surprise, she nearly fell over me before moving to the podium.

This left me with Pam, who looked terribly worried about taking a gamble on me for such a big event. I tried to act very together and not at all like a lady who wears dirty underwear and styles her hair with a golf pencil. She asked when I planned to drive back. I told her that since I didn't sleep well anymore, I'd just get up whenever I decided to stop trying to sleep and head back

home. To which she responded, "Oh, you're in 'the change . . . '"
and then pretty much started in where Miriam had left off.

When it was time for me to do my thing, I took the podium.
The clanking of plates, silverware, and chairs, combined with
people talking to their table mates while I was speaking, was
extremely distracting. I offered a silent prayer for help in staying
focused and for having the right words, the words they needed
to hear, come out of my mouth.

I began by sharing Jaclyn's story of her life in the orphanage—a
tale of pain and suffering and almost unbearable grief, but also a
story of the triumph of love and hope. As I did, the tenor in the
ballroom shifted until silence reigned. Not a clink, not a movement, not a sound. The crowd was in my hands in a way I had
never experienced.

Afterward, I made my way to the back of the room to sign
books, assisted by a plucky lady named Alice, who was all of about
four foot seven and ninety years old. A line formed of people who
thanked me for coming and then told me how Jaclyn's story had
touched their hearts in some way. They asked for pictures with
me. They hugged me. They told me their own stories.

A friend of Miriam's told me why I'd been brought here to
honor her. In her early twenties, Miriam and her husband had
traveled to India. While there, a captivating twelve-year-old boy
begged to shine her shoes. As the conversation unfolded and she
pressed him to share his story, she found out his parents had sold
him to a businessman as an indentured servant. In exchange for
shoe-shining all day, he was given a mat to sleep on and one
meal a day.

Miriam tried to forget the boy, but she couldn't. She ended up "purchasing" his freedom. She then enrolled him in a British boarding school and paid for his education and living expenses until he was grown. She asked for only one thing in return—the shoe-shine kit. She brought it home with her—determined he would never use it again—and displayed it prominently in her home as a continual reminder of how blessed she was to be an American and to have the life of comfort she claimed as her birthright. It also served as a reminder of those who are not so fortunate. She vowed sixty years ago never to forget. She never did. She spent all the days of her life, in any way she could, doing volunteer work to make a small part of this world right. And she was still doing that at the age of eighty-five.

I noticed a woman in her seventies hanging back from the rest, waiting for the others in line to go. I steeled my heart, knowing from experience that there was something powerful this person wanted to share with me.

The woman approached me shyly and told me she'd spent her life as an adoption social worker, trying to find homes for foster kids. She locked her eyes on mine. "I was a foster child myself. No one adopted me. *No one ever wanted me.*" I saw in her eyes a look I'd seen on hundreds of tiny faces in orphanages on the other side of the world. The pain of that look never left my heart. To see it in her eyes was almost more than I could bear. I had no words to say in response—no words big enough to fill this cavernous hole in her heart. I simply opened my arms and held her.

As we stood there hugging, she whispered in my ear, "Thank you for being the voice for the kids no one wants. They have no voice of their own." She pulled away from my embrace and looked me in the eye. "Please, don't ever stop."

I had been intending to do just that. I thought of the past twenty-eight months of my life and how much I had wanted to be done with the dizzying schedule. The finish line was close. I was sure I'd feel tremendous relief when it was over.

But instead, I felt sadness. My mission was bigger than just writing a book or sharing a story. It was about never resting until all the children who are left behind—the countless kids whose pictures aren't on anyone's fireplace mantel, whose hope is measured in direct proportion to our advocacy for them—have a future.

Sometimes angels prod us forward in the form of seventy-year-old former foster children who never outgrew the pain of not being chosen.

You and I can't do anything about the millions of kids all over the world who live outside the protection of families. The problem is too big. And we are too small. But Jaclyn once told me that when she lived in China, she never saw the little boy she cared for smile. Not once. Jaclyn never stopped advocating for him, pleading for him, begging for him, hoping for him. Today you can't wipe the smile off his face. He is handsome, healthy, smart, and athletic. He was chosen. And every time I see him smile, I am reminded of this powerful truth: we can all do for one.

If Jaclyn could do it, you can do it. Use your voice. Use your feet. Use your money. Use your talents. Use your energy. Do for one. And don't ever stop.

I can't live in the company of complacency anymore. Because I've discovered my truth—the one thing I know for sure. And discovering our own truth is one of the most powerful gifts of life.

Speaking your truth out loud is liberating. It's exhilarating. It's freeing. Being true to the things you know in your heart are right is the only way to fully experience life. That's why powerful truth is the most satisfying gift of all.

The Tenth Gift

Partners and Protectors

$\mathcal{M}$aybe the greatest gift in life is that we don't have to experience it alone. Most joyful experiences center around those we love—our partners, friends, family. Fun is not a solitary experience.

But what about the hard times? Are we meant to suffer in silence? To tamp down our pain? To suck it up? I don't think so. It is when we are in the deepest suffering that we most need our partners and protectors. In those dark moments, a partner grabs your hand and pulls you up. Grab that hand. Seize the precious gift of help when it's offered. And then pay it forward by looking for a chance to be that hand for another.

Life is not meant to be lived alone. We are not alone. Partners and protectors are there to hold us up. And sometimes just to hold us. For this reason, partners and protectors are the most comforting gift of life.

Family is the people who stand with you in your darkest hour.

When you looked at the table of contents of this book, you may have thought, *Something's missing here. How can there be a book about the gifts of life that doesn't include any mention of family?* First let me assure you that the reason has nothing to do with the word *family* not starting with the letter *p*. But I did have my reasons; let me explain.

For many, family is the greatest gift of all. If you are one of those lucky ones, hold them close and make sure to tell them how much they mean to you (and not just on holidays). Tell them before it's too late. Tell them with the passion you'd feel if it were too late.

But for others, family is much more complicated. For some, family is the people they see when obligation motivates the invitation. The truth is that for many, home is the place where their deepest betrayals began, and a lifetime isn't long enough to heal the wounds that have been inflicted. Family members are supposed to love you most, understand you best, and stand by you always. When that doesn't happen, an emotional orphan is born—a person who has family, yet does not.

Years ago my dear friends Joyce and Larry faced a challenge that would try even the most devoted parents. Their twenty-something son came to them and said he had met the woman he wanted to marry. Good news, right? Then he added: oh, by the way, she isn't divorced from her first husband yet. And: oh, by the way, she's pregnant. Oh. Because this is a loving and deeply religious family, Joyce and Larry focused on how to bubble-wrap these two hurting people in compassion. They avoided lectures. This young couple knew they were in a major mess-up. They didn't need to hear that. What they needed was support in untangling their tangled mess.

When the day of the nuptials finally arrived, the bride was nearly nine months pregnant. Joyce and Larry planned the wedding at their home. My girls and I eagerly offered to help. We were given the honor of decorating for the event.

I gamely agreed to wrap ribbon bows on the chair backs—even though the closest I'd ever come to craft activities with my kids was wrapping Scotch tape around their fingers. My heart was in the right place; my fingers, not so much. Everyone tried not to comment on the limp, awkward tilting of my best-effort bows.

Other friends helped with the reception meal, setting up chairs, arranging floral bouquets, setting tables, and washing dishes and picking up the trash afterward. It was a celebration of love and life and new beginnings.

At the end of the evening, as I watched friends helping with the clean-up, I realized that no one from either Joyce's or Larry's family was there. Larry was one of nine children, and Joyce had three sisters. Where were they? I couldn't imagine how much it must hurt not to have any family there.

Because Joyce and I are so close that we can speak the truth to each other, even when it's painful, I asked her, "Where's your family?"

"Look around this room," she replied.

I gazed at a small army of people helping and smiling and joyfully making this event a special occasion with their hearts full of love, not judgment. Protective of those whom they cherished. Partners in whatever needed to be done. And then Joyce added quietly: "My family *is* here."

In difficult times, true relationships are revealed. When you're in your darkest moment, look for the ones who stand shoulder to shoulder with you. Hold tight to those who love you no matter what. And embrace them as family.

When you find someone who touches your soul, grab that person's hand and run into the elephants.

Years ago I took my then two-year-old, Kate, to a friend's house in the neighborhood. I wanted him to see how adorable she looked in her Halloween costume. Several lights were on inside, so I knew he was home. I rang the bell. No one came to the door. I rang again. Still no answer. I peeked through the glass in the door and saw his shoes—my friend, a 6'3", 220-lb. grown man, was hiding behind his couch!

When I stopped laughing, I yelled out, "It's just me!" He came to the door, clearly mortified. He explained with embarrassment that since they never had any trick-or-treaters, he didn't have any candy. So he panicked when the doorbell rang and thought that if he pretended no one was there, whoever it was would go away.

This is pretty much how I acted after my divorce—hiding behind my couch, pretending no one was home, and hoping others would go away.

And then in a pretty ordinary life that had never glimpsed anything close to fairy godmothers or glass slippers, something extraordinary happened—my Prince Charming showed up. He arrived a little late, in my opinion, but no worse for wear. And suddenly I fell into a real-life fairytale—a breathless, heart-pounding love that I knew from the beginning would end in happily-ever-after. The kind of love you see in corny movies where people fall head-over-heels for each other the moment they meet, and you walk out of the theatre thinking how silly that was because that never happens in real life.

Years ago an acquaintance told me about her forty-three blissful years of happiness married to a man she had known for six weeks. I thought she was lucky their relationship worked out, because it was nuts to think anyone could get to know a person in six weeks well enough to love that person for a lifetime. But what happened between me and my Prince Charming was that kind of love. Most people don't understand it because they've never felt it. I certainly hadn't. Until it happened to me. On our third date, we shopped for wedding bands.

When we were together, I couldn't take my eyes off of his face. Every minute was treasured even more because a six-hour drive separated us—he lived in Chicago; I lived in Detroit. But for us, one day together was worth more than a lifetime with any other. I knew his thoughts before he expressed them. I felt as if I could see into his soul. It was exhilarating.

When we were with others, we tried to tamp down our love and devotion to each other—mostly so they didn't gag, but also because we knew how rare this was and that those who have never known this kind of love can't begin to fathom it. We knew how crazy it sounded that we were hopelessly in love after three dates, and we wanted to be respectful of the time that others needed to understand.

Though it might seem too soon for others, to us it seemed like an eternity of waiting. We wanted to publicly declare our love and commitment to each other. However, as a mom with three daughters, I realized this was a group decision. This was not just my life; it was *our* life.

A few months earlier, Kate, twelve years old at the time, entertained fantasies of us becoming a mother-daughter dating duo à la the Gilmore Girls. She had told me on the way to school one morning her list of what *we* were looking for in a potential new mate. Her list consisted of:

1. Someone who doesn't yell.
2. Someone who likes kids. A lot.
3. Someone who isn't a policeman. Maybe a teacher would be good (see #2 above).
4. Someone who will go to the movies with us even if it is a stupid, boring, kids' movie.
5. Someone who isn't *too* old.
6. Someone with a nice son around Kate's age, maybe a few years older.
7. Someone with a boat.

Then she generously asked me what was on *my* list. As I hadn't even thought about the topic, I had to punt. "Someone who is kind and nice and loves us all a lot," I said. She nodded. "And maybe sorta cute?" I added. She rolled her eyes and sighed. "Well, if that matters to you . . . but it's kind of superficial, don't you think?"

So when Prince Charming showed up in the form of a former elementary school teacher named Joe who was crazy about kids, loved kids' movies, excelled in patience, wasn't *too* old, had *two* nice sons, and even owned a boat, I figured he was a slam dunk for all of us. And for Kate and Christy, he was. When the door shut after they first met him, a visit in which he charmed them with cool card tricks and fun games he knew, Kate said immediately, "Reel him in, Mom. He's perfect!"

And then there was Jaclyn. I tried to prepare Joe for what a challenging child she could be, but he dismissed all my warnings. "I used to teach fifth grade," he said. "I know ten-year-olds."

So I sat back and watched him struggle to understand a child who defies understanding. But he didn't cry uncle. Instead he worked tirelessly to show her that he could be trusted and that he was good and kind and honorable and loving. And fun too.

Unfortunately, he was stymied in his efforts by an early tactical error. We stopped one day for ice cream cones at McDonald's, and I pulled a five-dollar bill out of my purse to pay for them. Jaclyn frowned; she never forgot it. Given the early deprivation in her life, food was critical to her security, and having a dad who provided for her was more so. How could she trust a guy who didn't pay?

Later, Jaclyn tried to pin her reluctance to commit to Joe on a technicality. "Mom, isn't there a limit to how many different hair colors you can have in one family?" I was blonde, Kate a brunette, my two Asian daughters had black hair, and now I hoped to add a red-haired man to the mix.

I stifled a chuckle and answered, "No. There are no limits on family."

She wasn't convinced.

When Joe had pretty much given up ever winning her over, it happened. One night when I was putting her to bed, she added at the end of her prayer, "And thank you, God, for making my mom happy again." She opened her eyes and said to me solemnly, "Mom, it's okay with me if you want to get married."

The final obstacle resolved!

But then I got cold feet. What if I failed again? If he betrayed me, I would never recover. If he left me, I would not be able to go on living. What if he changed? What if I changed? What if happily-ever-after really did only exist in fairy tales?

Fear that originated from the dark abyss of my failed relationship landed squarely between me and my future happiness.

Being the pragmatic business school graduate I am, I tried to reassure myself by doing what my professors had taught me to do when faced with a critical decision: make a list of pros and cons.

The pros of marrying Joe were easy:

1. He could pick out a gift I loved without my having to show him a picture, rip out a catalog page, write down the size and color, and highlight the phone number to call.
2. He kept a bag of Twizzlers in his car for me, knowing I was a secret Twizzler addict.
3. I could take him to a boring work event where he didn't know a single person, and he didn't complain. He mingled incredibly well. Afterward, my colleagues asked where I found him, because he was the most charming guy they'd ever met.
4. He acted like he never noticed that I was covered in cellulite, had a saggy rear end, and looked every bit my age.
5. He was thoughtful of others, even strangers. When we were walking in the city one rainy day and he saw a little

girl and her mom get out of a cab in front of a huge, deep puddle, he walked into the puddle and lifted the little girl over it so she didn't get her party shoes wet.

6. He was loyal beyond belief. When I had a cancer scare, I told him I didn't want him to marry me if I did have cancer. Who would want to be married to a bald, disfigured, sallow-skinned, barfing person? He told me he would marry me anyway because the part of me he loved wouldn't be disfigured, sallow-skinned, and barfing. And if I lost my hair I should get a red wig to match his hair color and we could act like one of those dorky matching figure-skating couples.

7. He cared about my feelings, desires, and goals. When I told him I wanted to adopt another baby (just to mess with him), and he asked me if I was serious, and I said yes, he said the best part of his life was being a dad, and if this was something I really wanted, he'd be excited about it. (And then I felt crummy because I didn't really want another baby.)

8. He didn't badmouth anyone. When I finished yet another tirade about the wrongs in my life and invited him to join in the pity party by telling me three things he disliked about his ex-wife, he said he tried really hard not to do that because she gave him two wonderful kids.

I didn't need the list to tell me what I already knew—he was almost too good to be true. I didn't need my friends telling me that he was the rarest of all men. I didn't need my kids teasing me to know that he was the one who made my heart sing.

I pulled out another sheet of paper and wrote "cons" at the top. There was only one, but it was a biggie: fear.

A wedding was planned. And cancelled. Fear had wrapped itself around my heart, and I could not break free of its hold. I broke up with him for a while, insisting we should date others. He told me I could do that if I wanted to, but he wouldn't because he knew I was *the one* and he would wait for me forever.

I did date someone else. A handsome, charming, successful man I met, ironically, in my church parking lot. It was almost as if God parked him there to teach me a lesson. When I went out with this guy, I always came home wondering why I felt so empty inside. He was gorgeous. He made me laugh. He brought flowers. He was entertaining. But he wasn't Joe.

Cindy and her love, Joe

Joe gently urged me to talk to a therapist. I hadn't even considered doing this. After all, I was a trained psychologist. What could I possibly learn from a therapist?

To please Joe, I went. I did my best to swallow my annoyance at the way he kept interrupting my monologue of past failures with his advice.

But then he told me something that haunted me for days afterward. "How many great loves does a person get in a lifetime?" I shook my head mutely. "I've asked that question of many people in the later years of their life," he went on. "The consensus is that one great love is the most anyone can hope for. Two if you're very lucky. Sadly, many never know a great love at all."

I nodded, counting in my head. I had burned one chance at great love years ago when I was in college. I never thought I'd feel anything close to it again. Now I had something even better.

"You and Joe have a great love," the therapist continued. "If you walk away from it, be prepared for the fact that you may never find it again."

Then he leaned forward and told me a parable that resonated with such truth that it looped endlessly in my mind afterward. "There once was a field in Africa that small animals had to cross to continue on their journey. There were two paths out of the field. One path was blocked by a herd of elephants. The other path was blocked by lions snoozing peacefully in the sun. When the small animals entered the field, the elephants joyfully acknowledged their presence by wildly flapping their ears and braying loudly. The small animals saw these massive beings and heard their loud noise and ran as fast as they could in the opposite direction . . . where the lions, no longer sleeping in the sun, pounced on them and devoured them."

He then explained the moral of the story. "When you run from what you fear in this life—a broken heart, commitment, being hurt again—a part of you dies."

It was then I realized that if I ran away from Joe, my soul would die.

And I thought, too, of Jaclyn and her dark past. Years ago in China, she took a deep breath and summoned all her four-year-old courage and ran into the elephants. She reached out for the hand of a stranger she was now expected to call "mama." Most amazing of all, she trusted me with her heart—a heart that had been trampled on by the one who was supposed to love her most. If she could love again—if she could trust her soul to another—how could I not?

A few weeks later, the girls and I flew to Orlando for a weekend celebration of my fiftieth birthday. When we got off the plane, we found a handsome man in a tuxedo, holding red roses, an amazing ring, and a big sign that said, "Cindy Champnella: Will You Marry Me?" I was no longer afraid. But just in case, Joe had planned an intimate wedding on the beach for the very next day.

In the late afternoon, with our five children in a circle of love around us, my partner, my protector, my great love held my hand, and I ran into the elephants.

Fairytale ending, right? Not quite. Jaclyn refused to wait in the air-conditioned van with the rest of us when the minister was late in arriving. And even though it was a hot day in Florida, she refused to drink "yucky drinking-foundation water," so she got

Joe and Cindy with their five children at their beach side wedding

dehydrated. Just as I was saying my wedding vows, she hollered out, "Mom, I don't feel too good. I think I'm going to throw up!"

I released my beloved's hand, excused myself from the minister, and said to her, "I'm kind of in the middle of something right now. Can you just hang on?"

My wedding came to a hasty conclusion, but I can't wait for *her* wedding.

You can change everything if you grab the hand of the one left behind.

In the struggling urban school district where I was an administrator, the day I dreaded most was when we had to tell the seniors who would *not* be graduating. In our district, we dubbed this day "Black Tuesday."

I wanted to shake some of these kids for not having tried harder. Others had done their best but had still fallen short. Some of them would never try again. They were the ones I most wanted to cry for.

Facing those students was hard enough, but nothing compared to seeing the disappointment in the faces of their parents, many of whom had pinned all their hopes and dreams on their children.

One year we had a student on the "not graduating" list because he didn't pass Physical Education. This young man was hugely obese. And one of the requirements in P.E. was completing a half mile on the track. You were supposed to run, but walking was allowed. Even though he had been told he could take as long as he needed, this student refused to try. The P.E. teacher was furious about his stubborn refusal to even attempt it and failed him in the course. If you didn't make it around the track, you failed P.E. If you failed P.E., you didn't graduate. The rules were the rules.

I came into school the Saturday following "Black Tuesday" to work on a project I hadn't been able to get to during the week. My office overlooked the track. As I glanced out the window, I saw two figures making their way around the track very slowly; I recognized one as the high school principal. He was a man who didn't accept failure. I found out later that he had quietly approached this young man and had told him to meet him at the track on Saturday when everyone else was gone. He told him that he didn't care if they were there all day and all night, but the two of them together were going to make it around that track. He walked every step of the way alongside him. With the encouragement, support, and tenaciousness of this remarkable principal, the boy made it . . . and he graduated.

I never asked him how many kids he had refused to allow to fail over the years. But I never forgot him. And I suspect that young man never did, either. We never forget the people who walk beside us, literally and figuratively, when we think we can't do it, when we don't believe in ourselves. But maybe the one who benefited most from his kindness was the principal. Because when you extend your hand, your heart, your life, your-self . . . your walk through life changes. And if you are tenacious enough, if you refuse to give up on those who have given up on themselves, you can even become the difference between failure and triumph.

> In your darkest moment, reach one hand up and the other hand out . . . and there will be a hand to hold onto.

My husband, Joe, is terrified of snakes. Like most pronounced fears, this one has its origin in childhood. When he was five years old, his dad and older brothers were digging a long, deep ditch to put in new sewer lines on their farm. Joe and his younger brother, too little to help, were playing in the ditch. Joe was running barefoot when he glanced down and saw a snake slith-ering directly in his path. He screamed, terrified and panicked, desperate to get out of a ditch that was shoulder high on both sides—much too deep for him to crawl out of on his own. Sud-denly, he was lifted by two strong arms. His father had heard his cries and, in one fell swoop, brought him out of terror and onto the firm ground of safety.

I think this is how many people see God. When they're in trouble, they expect to feel those strong arms reaching down from above and rescuing them.

I see God differently. I think He uses a gentle nudge, a whisper, a nagging prod to move into our path the one person we need in that moment to get us through it. He uses all of us as His hands and His hugs. There's just us—there is no plan B.

Our protectors and partners are ordinary, everyday people who come into our lives—some just for a season—and hear the hurt behind our words, give us the advice we need to hear, love us without judgment, and make us smile again. It can be a teacher, a student, a book-club buddy, a neighbor, a colleague. Sometimes it's your sister. Or someone you've chosen to be your sister. But whatever the relationship, if you reach out your hand for strength, there will be a hand to hold.

Sometimes that hand belongs to a child. When four-year-old Jaclyn lived in a Chinese orphanage, the staff there had the impossible task of figuring out how to care for nearly four hundred children with limited budgets and even more limited staff. If the children were older than three, they were expected to pitch in by doing certain jobs. Jaclyn's responsibility was to care for two small toddlers.

As she came to trust me, Jaclyn admitted that she had stolen food when she lived in the orphanage. Her thievery was not for herself but for the toddlers she protected. She understood that doing the right thing sometimes means breaking the rules. That took me a long time to figure out.

I've heard others criticize the orphanage staff for allowing four-year-old Jaclyn to become protector to two small toddlers. I see it differently. Her love for these little ones kept her heart intact. She needed to love as much as they needed her love. If she hadn't had others who needed her, to give her life purpose, I'm not sure who she would be today. She certainly would have been remarkably different from the incredibly loving child who became my daughter.

That's the beautiful irony of love. Whenever we reach out our hands, whenever we step out to protect, whenever we commit to becoming a true partner to someone, whenever we throw out a lifeline, the life we save is our own.

The Eleventh Gift

Prayer

$\mathcal{W}$hen my youngest daughter, Christy, got her first cell phone as a gift for her ninth birthday, it became a lifeline between us. She called me as soon as she got home from school. She called me whenever she was visiting a friend. If she had a sleepover, she called me before she went to bed and as soon as she woke up. Occasionally, she even called me in the middle of the night. Often she had nothing new to report but only called to tell me she loved me and to hear the reassurance of that same love returned.

Thinking about how much I loved to hear from her, how good I felt when I knew she wanted to talk with me, how this ongoing connection showed me the important place I had in her life, gave me a huge "aha moment" about prayer.

Before this revelation, I had prayed in short bursts. I didn't want to bother God with the mundane details of my life, thinking He was too busy sorting out more important things like wars and deathbed confessions. I made my prayers brief and succinct, only asking for divine assistance when I was at my wit's end.

But when I realized how much I loved hearing from *my* child, how much I relished even the smallest contact, how much I rejoiced in knowing she was thinking loving thoughts of me, I realized how flawed my thinking had been. God wants to hear from us. He wants to comfort us even when our fears are trivial.

He wants us to know, and really feel, that He is there watching over us—just a simple prayer away.

Prayer is our source of strength. It is our rock during the storms of life. But too many of us use prayer as our Plan B. If all else fails, we pray. We've got it all backward. Prayer is meant to be our Plan A—the place we go to for directions to the right path instead of the place we go for help when we crash.

To pray is to unleash the power of the universe. We have the ability to speak to the One who created life.

But first you must believe.

To really understand faith, you must believe like a child.

Soon after I became a mom, I learned how inadequate my explanations of faith were. One misty, late-spring evening when the girls were young, they sat in the car with me as we drove back home after visiting a friend. It had been a long car ride, and Kate and Christy had fallen asleep in the backseat. But I couldn't tear my eyes off the brilliant rainbow that stretched majestically over the road. I pointed it out to five-year-old Jaclyn, who exclaimed with delight over the brilliant colors she could identify.

This prompted me to ask her if she knew that the rainbow symbolized God's promise not to ever destroy the earth by flood again. I launched into telling her the story of Noah's ark. Because she was in the backseat, I couldn't see her ever-growing panic. Jaclyn was horrified by the story and, as usual, peppered me with rapid-fire questions.

"Why did God get so mad?"

"What bad things did the people do?"

"How long did the animals stay in there?"

I hadn't stopped to think how frightening the thought of a worldwide flood might be to a small child. As her anxious questions poured out, I reassured her over and over that this flood happened a long, long time ago. Hundreds of years ago, in fact. And she didn't have to worry about it ever happening again.

That left her with only one question: "Mama, did you get wet in the flood?"

~~~~~~

I sometimes have a hard time addressing my children's questions, because the answers evade me too.

I've wondered from time to time what the hereafter will be like. I've even bought books written by those who've had near-death experiences, hoping to get a peek into the next life. Little did I realize that I had an expert on the subject right in my own home.

Since Jaclyn seemed to be an authority on everything else, I guess I shouldn't have been surprised that she believed she knew all about this topic as well.

I discovered this one cold, rainy Michigan morning when the girls were all snuggled together in my bed.

"I want to stay home from preschool today," three-year-old Christy stated. "I want to stay in my jammies all day and cuddle." She burrowed down into the covers.

"Christ-ta-tee, you have to stop being such a baby," five-year-old Jaclyn said with a hint of annoyance. I figured Jaclyn had reason to be irritated. After all, in her former life she had a fairly responsible job at the orphanage caring for two toddlers; she didn't abide slackers at any age. But this wasn't the reason for her annoyance.

"Christ-ta-tee, Mama's *very* old. She's going to die pretty soon, and Katie and I are not going to take care of you."

I quickly piped in to defend myself. "I'm not *that* old. I've got a few good years yet."

Jaclyn looked skeptically at the dark circles under my eyes. With seeming reluctance, she modified her prediction. "Christ-ta-tee, Mama's going to die when you sixteen. Then she go up to heaven. She still can see you then, but you can't see her."

Christy burrowed farther into the covers. "I don't ever want to go to heaven. I want to stay here!"

"There's no goose bumps in heaven," Jaclyn said in her most persuasive voice, looking at the raised bumps on her sister's arm. "It's warm all the time there."

Christy wasn't convinced. "I not cold, I itchy," she said, furiously scratching her eczema.

"There's no 'itch-yous' in heaven, either," Jaclyn, the consummate saleswoman, said. "There even no such thing as chicken pops!"

Christy still looked skeptical.

"In heaven, God do all the cooking for everybody. I think it hard for him because his fingers are as big as our heads. And God got a great big huge washing machine. Every morning he give us nice clean white clothes to wear."

"What if we get mud on them?" Christy asked.

"Christ-ta-tee, there no such thing as mud in heaven. Why you think God make the rain go down, not up? To keep the mud on the ground!"

I guess God *had* thought of everything. I was left wondering, though, why He hadn't come up with a way to get out of cooking and laundry for all of us. On the other hand, an eternal future without either one did sound heavenly.

~~~~~

The sister dynamics in our home spilled over into the mysteries of faith. Kate instructed Jaclyn, and Jaclyn, in turn, clarified things for Christy.

Right before Easter, seven-year-old Kate chided Jaclyn about her excitement over the upcoming visit from the Easter Bunny.

"You know Easter isn't just about the bunny and egg hunts," she said sternly. "It's about the story of Jesus dying." She then proceeded to relate her version of the biblical story. "After Jesus died and was in the tomb, some ladies came and rolled aside the enormous, huge stone."

You go, girls! I smiled to myself, thinking of those long-ago women.

"They had to get in there so they could put some seasoning on Him."

I guess He just marinated in there until Easter.

Kate also tried to instruct Christy. Being small in stature, Christy had a difficult time getting off the last step of the bus she rode to preschool. One day, on her leap from the bottom step, she fell face first on the cement and got a nasty scrape on her tiny nose. She was very self-conscious about the scab, and I overheard her asking her wise older sister, Kate, when the scab would go away.

"I really don't know," Kate said solemnly. "The only one who knows for sure is God."

That was all the prompting Christy needed. She lifted her head and said, "God, how long before my scab comes off?" She then cocked her head and listened expectantly.

A moment later, Kate asked, "Well, what did He say?"

"I can't hear him," Christy grumbled. "He needs to use his outdoor voice."

~~~~~

As her third birthday approached, Christy finally started to talk in real sentences. I had begun to despair about her language development, especially since Jaclyn took it upon herself early on to teach Christy to talk. Jaclyn, who hadn't learned English until after she was adopted at the age of four, often mispronounced words, then insisted that Christy repeat them after her.

Jaclyn even tried to teach Christy colors before she knew them herself. "Christ-ta-tee, say white," she prompted while holding up something pink. I figured it would be years before I could undo all this helpful instruction from Jaclyn.

But children seem to have their own special way of communicating. When Christy said something I couldn't understand, Jaclyn often successfully interpreted for me.

One night as I was putting the girls to bed, Christy insistently demanded something, and though I tried to understand, I had no idea what she was saying. She repeatedly howled her request, so I prevailed upon Jaclyn to interpret. Jaclyn leaned over from her bed to the trundle where her sister slept and asked, "What you want, Christ-ta-tee?"

After the garbled request was repeated, Jaclyn told me, "She wants to say her 'Dear God.'"

So I knelt down to hear Christy's prayer. Her list of "God blesses" grew long, including many inanimate objects in addition to people. Finally, impatient Jaclyn leaned over the railing and said in a loud voice, "Amen!"

You tell her, Jaclyn. I'm sure God appreciated her intervention to keep the prayer line moving.

~~~~~

Jaclyn wasn't content to just boss around those in our family. She was becoming quite the leader at church too.

One Sunday our church had an informal service featuring some folk gospel sung to the accompaniment of guitars. Our staid older congregation sat stiffly singing the songs. Not Jaclyn. Although she didn't know the lyrics, she rhythmically clapped to the beat. To her disappointment, it did not catch on, but this did not dampen her enthusiasm. At the end of the singing, when the other members ended with a reverent "Amen," Jaclyn gave her own version of that term by singing out, "The end!"

Next came the Lord's Prayer. While the rest of the congregation was saying, "Deliver us from evil," Jaclyn yelled out, "Deliver us from *people*!" As I reflected on the source of the evil I'd known, I wanted to echo this sentiment myself.

After prayers, the minister made an announcement. "Today is a special occasion—it's Mrs. Scott's ninety-ninth birthday." The congregation murmured. Jaclyn leapt up onto the pew and peered around the church, trying to catch a glimpse of this icon.

"Where is she?" Jaclyn asked.

"She isn't here," her father said in an embarrassed whisper.

"She die?"

I guess if you're already ninety-nine and you can't make it to church, it's a logical question to ask, but titters broke out all around us.

Christy, however, was not tolerating this irreverent distraction. "Be quiet, Jaclyn," she said, straining to hear the minister's next words. "I can't hear what God's saying!"

Guess our minister got a big promotion.

~~~~~

Jaclyn changed the way I believed by showing me faith beyond what I had ever experienced. Living with Jaclyn that first year after I adopted her was like living with a very short mother who had had her baby ripped from her arms. She never stopped talking about Xiao Xiao, the child she'd cared for in the orphanage. Memories of him crowded into both times of joy and sorrow in our lives. She was like a beacon of light illuminating my understanding of what it was like to live in an orphanage. She could not forget him. She would not let me forget either.

Her desperation caused her to ask every adult in her life for help in finding a mama for her baby. Given the complexity of the bureaucracy that trapped him, both in China and in the complicated international adoption regulations in the US, the prospects were dismal. When she had exhausted herself, asking every adult she knew for help, and not seeing any promises being made in return, she turned to God.

I prayed with my children before bed every night. But in China, Jaclyn had never been exposed to anything of faith, so I wasn't sure what, if anything, she understood.

Jaclyn understood a lot more than I thought.

One night, after I finished praying, to my surprise she began to pray. The request to bring her baby to America was, predictably, the first prayer she uttered.

I had always thought of faith as a lifelong process. What she taught me is that faith is as simple as believing with your whole heart in something you can't see or understand. She believed God would help her find a mama for Xiao Xiao. She also believed God would help him not to be afraid in the darkness where he languished.

Hearing that simple prayer, night after night, had a profound effect on me. I realized that Jaclyn asked God for nothing for herself, but that all her prayers contained pleas for a mama for Xiao Xiao. It ripped a hole in my heart every time I heard her prayers; I could only imagine how her innocent words and her trusting faith impacted the heavenly Father.

Her faith taught me something about the power of prayer. It multiples. It multiplies in an explosive manner.

Not long after I began to share her quest for her baby through e-mails to my circle of friends, those messages were forwarded. Daily e-mails arrived from people I didn't even know:

"My prayer circle in New York is praying for Xiao Xiao."

"My mother and I pray for Jaclyn and Xiao Xiao every day."

"My daughter and daughter-in-law ask me constantly if there's any word about Jaclyn's baby."

A family in England wrote, "We have prayed that God would not forsake him."

I was reminded of Matthew 17:19, which says, "If you have faith as a grain of mustard seed . . . nothing shall be impossible unto you."

Over time, hearing Jaclyn's pleas changed me. Xiao Xiao became the dearest child on earth to me. He invaded my heart. I thought I was beyond falling in love again. But I did.

He was once just another nameless, faceless, family-less child in a myriad of lost children. But now, his pictures sat on my dresser and on my mantel. They belonged there as rightfully as the pictures of my own children.

As I continued to write about Jaclyn and her baby, and my e-mails to friends and family continued to be forwarded to others, the circle of those who loved him grew. Xiao Xiao may have thought Jaclyn had abandoned him the same way his birth mother had, but she never did. Not even for a day. She made many others pray for him, hope for him, and care about him.

People of various religious beliefs from different countries virtually held hands through cyberspace and formed a chain of faith that circled the globe. In many ways, and in different languages, they called on God to help two small children be reunited. And God, in his mercy and grace, made the impossible possible. I'm sure He smiled down from heaven when He watched a reunion that defied possibility occur just fifteen months after Jaclyn was adopted, when she marched back into that orphanage and grabbed the hand of her dear baby, Xiao Xiao.

Faith defies logic. And prayer opens the door for faith to work. It can make the impossible possible.

Our choices reflect our priorities.

After living in the pecking order of an orphanage environment, Jaclyn had a wariness of children who were older or bigger than she was, but she had great compassion and empathy for those who were smaller. When she heard her younger sister, Christy, crying, Jaclyn would immediately launch into a soothing mother-tone. "It's all right, baby. Jack-win here." As a result, Christy went to Jaclyn whenever she needed assistance.

As the Christmas holiday neared the first year after I adopted Jaclyn, a visiting friend pointed out to me that there was a new addition to the nativity scene set up on our living room coffee table. When I saw what had been added—a tiny doll-baby bottle—I knew who the culprit was. When I asked the girls who had done this, Jaclyn confessed. "Oh, Mama," she said, "I didn't want baby Jesus to be hungry."

Jaclyn next to the nativity scene where she added a bottle for baby Jesus

Who else would have worried about caring for the Christ child?

A few weeks later, Jaclyn's school sponsored a holiday craft fair. The children were encouraged to attend so they could make crafts as holiday gifts for family members. High school students ushered them through the various stations.

Jaclyn was proud of the seven crafts she completed. She hid them from me so I would be surprised at gift-exchange time. But at bedtime one night I noticed a white felt banner hanging from her desk. On it were brightly decorated gingerbread men. Jaclyn saw me looking at it and said, "That one is my favorite. I love it so much! Can I keep it?"

I recalled the answer my mother used when I was little to teach me how to make my own choices. Though I'd loathed it at the time, I tried it on Jaclyn. "Everything you make is yours. It's up to you to decide who you would like to have each item." The next day the banner disappeared.

Jaclyn and Kate wrapped their presents and stuck gift tags on them. I was curious as to who would end up with the banner Jaclyn cherished. I wondered who, of all those she loved, would claim that special place in her heart.

Jaclyn picked up the wrapped gift that contained her favorite gingerbread banner and said, "Mama, this one is for Jesus. It's His birthday, and you always get special gifts on your birthday."

Kate scoffed at her sister. "How are you going to get it to Jesus up in heaven?"

As always, Jaclyn had a plan. "When we see Santa Claus, I going to give it to him to put in his bag. He can give it to Jesus. He know where everybody live!"

I was glad I had Jaclyn to remind me of who should be first in our hearts—at Christmastime and always.

For many, their family of origin is a disappointment.
But there is one family in which we are
all loved and accepted and welcome.

During our first year with Jaclyn, much of our family life seemed to be on hold as we focused on the fate of her baby in

China, Xiao Xiao. When the closest thing she had to a biological sibling became part of our extended family, Jaclyn believed in miracles with all her heart. So did I.

I had delayed plans for Jaclyn's baptism until this important person from her past was here to participate in the celebration. Now that he was home, I told her we were going to have her baptized.

I struggled to explain to Jaclyn the significance of this event. In our church, child baptism was a preparatory ceremony, signifying that the parents vowed to raise the child to walk in the way that leads to life. Jaclyn had numerous questions, but the most compelling was: "Can Xiao Xiao be there with me?" He was happy to oblige.

Our minister asked us to meet with him the day before the baptism so he could review the protocol with us. The girls trooped into his tiny study after dire warnings on the ride to the church to behave. Our minister had marked several Bible passages to share with us and also had some inspirational readings.

As he began to read aloud, Jaclyn and Christy spied a bright yellow children's chair in the corner. A tug-of-war ensued, and the stuffed bear that had been perched there was flung across the room.

Jaclyn set the small chair on top of an adult chair and climbed on. Christy wailed hysterically. The minister read in a louder voice. The rest of us tried to ignore the escalating volume.

As he ushered us out of the office, he told me, "After your baptism ceremony, I'm conducting a private one for a child who is bipolar. His parents are worried about his behavior. He's very unpredictable."

"Our child isn't bipolar," I replied, "but we're concerned about her behavior too. She is also very unpredictable." He nodded.

The next morning, Jaclyn stood shyly at the front of the church. She proudly clutched Xiao Xiao's hand tightly throughout the ceremony. Our family now felt complete.

This joyous occasion was followed by a celebratory lunch at Jaclyn's second-favorite restaurant—the local Chinese place. I had to veto her first choice: McDonald's.

I had thought that the significance of the day had escaped her. At bedtime, Jaclyn prayed her usual prayer: "Dear God, thank You and Jesus for bringing my baby here. I love him, and I take care of him always. He always be my baby." Then, after a moment of searching for the right expression of gratitude, she added, "Thank You, God, for letting me be in Your family."

At that moment I realized how inadequate my explanation had been. *Let* her be in God's family? Like all God's children, she had always been a charter member of the family. Could her life have brought her to this place if she had been anywhere but inside God's pocket all along?

God is still in the miracle business.

The day I adopted Christy was, without a doubt, the happiest day of my life. During our adoption trip in China, the guide took me to a temple and stated that it was customary to make a wish. I was stymied. Everything I had wished for, I held in my arms. I had no wishes left.

When I got back home from China, I took my precious baby to the pediatrician for a checkup. When I insisted on having many tests run, he chided me for being an overanxious mom. He said the baby was obviously healthy. But he reluctantly gave in to my determined insistence.

That weekend I went to brunch with my closest friends. I told them I was completely happy, maybe for the first time in my life. I joked about not saying that aloud because it was like inviting the plague.

The next day, when I got home from running errands, my answering machine was full of messages from my pediatrician's office, demanding with increasing insistence that I bring Christy in immediately.

Upon my arrival, I was greeted by a highly agitated pediatrician. He told me the blood test results indicated that Christy had active, chronic hepatitis B. Chronic hepatitis is linked to liver cancer which is often deadly. Given the severity of the disease, it was likely a maternal transmission . . . and probably the reason her birth mother couldn't keep her.

He told me he had reported her condition to the Center for Disease Control and that no one should feel safe handling her. I needed to wear gloves when I changed her diapers. I should warn everyone who came in contact with her. Then he added, with a muttered curse, "They shouldn't let these kids into the country!"

I stood there in stunned silence while my world crashed around me.

Then began my frantic and fruitless chase for help. When the Center for Disease Control contacted me, they made my pediatrician's dire warnings seem tame by comparison. They asked me question after question about issues like the extent of her sexual contact. ("Hello! This is a six-month-old baby!") This quickly deteriorated into threatening to report her disease to every caretaker she had, every babysitter, and every school she attended.

The only way I could protect her from being a pariah was by my silence. I kept this dark secret to myself, refusing to give in to tears. The truth was, my grief was too deep for tears.

In a quest for answers, I took Christy to three highly esteemed specialists. They were united in their opinion that her prognosis was grim. This was a disease for which there was no cure, no treatment, no hope.

I asked them all the same question: "How long will she live?" The first two specialists tap danced without giving me an answer. The third doctor specialized in internationally adopted children and was an adoptive mom herself. I appealed to the mother in her by saying I had to know the truth about her future. I needed to be prepared. She asked me if I was sure. When I nodded, she said that Christy would be lucky if she lived to age fifty. There was a 25 percent probability she'd die before the age of eighteen.

When I asked at what age she might develop liver cancer, the doctor replied that she currently had a seven-year-old in her practice who had it. Then she said the worst words anyone can hear from a physician: "I'm sorry."

Holding on to a flicker of hope, I had Christy evaluated for a clinical trial of a new drug. She was turned down for being too small. After reading websites where people reported on alternative treatments, I took her to a homeopathic healer who gave her drops under her tongue. Nothing changed.

I read scattered reports about people who had mysteriously seroconverted and become disease-free. I confronted one of the specialists with these reports. He shook his head and looked at me with pity. "No one with this disease at the level Christy has it while younger than one year old has ever seroconverted," he said with finality. "It isn't possible."

I let go of the last shred of hope.

There are two distinct groups of parents on this earth—those who have tasted the fear of losing their child and those who have not. There are no words big enough to gulf the chasm between these two groups, so I won't even attempt it. Except to say that if you are in the latter group, you should turn your face to the sky and whisper thanks to God every day for the gift of not knowing this unspeakable despair.

Christy, the child who was my greatest joy, had become my secret sorrow. I understood her prognosis as a fact in my rational mind, in the same way that I understood that the world could end during my lifetime. They were both possibilities too fearsome, too staggering, and too remote for me to comprehend. I could not understand what losing her would mean for me, because the magnitude of such a loss was unfathomable. I was only sure that even knowing her grim prognosis didn't make it possible to love her any less or to protect my heart against the eventual loss of her bright light from my life.

My Chinese friend Fong told me Christy would not have been eligible for adoption if her medical condition had been known in China. I was grateful that it was hidden.

Every day, every single day, I begged God for a miracle. If anyone ever deserved one, it was this child. But part of me understood why God might want her with Him. She was, in many ways, too precious for this earth.

Somehow this prognosis made me love Christy even more. I felt lucky to be her mother for whatever time we had together. I held her close, sure that my time with her was limited. I savored her sweetness, drinking in every moment with her, not comprehending how I would ever be able to live without her.

I asked my mother, a true prayer warrior, to pray for her, though I was vague about the details of her condition. I asked many others to pray as well. But as the years went by, I began to worry that I'd already used up a lifetime of favors by asking for His intervention in bringing Jaclyn's baby here. I never thought that a miracle would occur. It's not that I doubted God could cure Christy; I just didn't believe that He would. Miracles happened to others. Or not at all.

There are two ways to live life. We can live as if disaster is around every corner, cowering in fear, expecting the worst to happen. Or we can choose to turn our face to the light. I chose the latter.

As part of my plan to not dwell in dark possibilities, I stopped taking Christy for her biannual assessment. I had been told too many times by too many doctors that nothing could be done, so I saw no point in continuing to put her through this ordeal.

These visits only reinforced the feeling of hopelessness that I tried so hard to beat back.

In the spring of 2002, Christy began waking at night with heavy nosebleeds. The profuse bleeding soaked her bed clothes and terrified her. Those blood stains seemed to mock my fervent desire to block out the truth. Reluctantly, I took her to a new pediatrician, sure that this was a sign of her deteriorating condition. The doctor was worried too; she ordered new blood tests to be done.

The next weekend, I took the girls to Niagara Falls. When we arrived back home, the answering machine was full of messages. My heart sank as I played them back and realized that every call was from the pediatrician, insisting that I call immediately. Remembering the last time this had happened, I punched in her number with shaking fingers and a heavy heart.

She answered the phone breathless. "You won't believe this. I couldn't believe it myself. I went to the lab and personally checked all the results. I even had the blood rechecked. Three times. Christy has seroconverted. The disease is completely gone! There is no trace of it in her system."

Though I had begged God for this, I couldn't believe it was true. I was afraid to even say it out loud, sure that it was a mistake, the tests were a fluke, and we would be devastated again.

The doctor and I agreed to have her retested in ninety days to make sure. When the time came, I couldn't take her. I was too afraid to let go of this fine strand of hope.

Weeks later, shamed by a friend's gentle rebuke, I summoned all my courage and took Christy back in—without an appointment, before I lost my nerve. The test results again showed that she was fine. Normal. Healthy. These words were like music to my ears.

I asked to have the test results forwarded to the specialist who had told me he had never heard of such a thing.

The liver is the only organ that can regenerate. Over time, Christy regained the liver function she had lost. And the mysterious nosebleeds stopped; Christy never had another one. They had served their purpose—providing the crisis needed to have her retested so I could hear the best news imaginable.

Now, I ask again, do you believe?

Final Thoughts about the Power of Prayer

Prayer holds the key to releasing us from the bondage that comes from being unable to forgive ourselves. Sometimes it's easier to live with guilt and self-recriminations than to open ourselves up to the forgiveness that is freely available to all. God wants us to own our mistakes—and then release them.

There are no "do overs" in life. But there are "do betters." To say, "I need forgiveness and I'll do better," is to say, "I'm flawed and broken and have caused hurt. But tomorrow I want to try again." To know that you are forgiven and to release the guilt is to free yourself from the bondage of regret.

And if you don't know where to begin to leave your legacy, ask God to show you who needs help in their lives. Then listen for His whisper and reach out to those He brings into your path who need a helping hand. Remember them in your prayers too.

We usually pray for ourselves, our children, and our families, pretty much in that order. Then we're done. But research contains numerous studies that document that when strangers pray for other strangers, healings occur that defy understanding. The scientific community is bewildered by these results. I just smile.

Prayer is the simplest gift we can give to another. It requires no money, no wrapping paper, no wrangling at the mall for a parking spot. It only requires one thing: faith. This force that baffles scientists changes lives.

To pray for someone is the ultimate gift. It shows you care, that this person matters in your life. Because we all matter to God.

Give the gift of prayer to yourself too. Let it change your life . . . because prayer is the most powerful gift of life.

The Twelfth Gift

Peace

$\mathcal{T}$he thing we desire most in life is peace. Peace in the world. Peace in our workplaces. Peace in our families. Peace in our hearts. Why, then, is peace so elusive?

Many of us spend a lifetime wondering what is missing from our lives. The empty place within drives many midlife crises, job changes, divorces. Then we discover that we can change the place we live, the people we're with, our circumstances, and even ourselves, but still be miserable.

Ultimately, peace comes from acceptance. Accepting others without trying to change them. Accepting that many things in life are beyond our control. Accepting ourselves as flawed and unfinished but still worthy.

Peace begins when we let go of the past and forgive others. It comes full circle when we forgive ourselves. Peace comes to us when we stop agitating and breathe. When we stop pushing and start living. When we live in the moment instead of the future. When we recognize that life is unfurling exactly as it is supposed to. Peace comes to us when we accept that we are not in charge of life—ours or anyone else's.

Take people the way they come to you and love them.

In the struggling urban school district where I worked as an administrator, I often sat in classrooms observing teachers who were up for evaluation. I approached those times with a mixture of joy and dread. Nothing could brighten my day more than a six-year-old joyously coming up to me in the hallway and asking me to admire his newly painted birdhouse. But the needs of those inner-city children—and the teachers who bravely tried to meet those needs—were hard for even a seasoned veteran to witness.

I saw children shivering in thin T-shirts on days when the broken-down heating system refused to spit out any more than the smallest puffs of warm air. I saw a teacher hand her morning muffin to a child with a growling stomach who eyed it enviously. I saw kids whose parents always came late to pick them up after preschool. I watched helplessly as children as young as seven or eight were summoned home from school by their mothers to babysit younger siblings so the mothers could walk out the door to go who knows where.

So I shouldn't have been surprised the day I noticed a second-grade child trying to make herself invisible as she slid into her desk, several minutes late, wearing ratty, threadbare pajamas. She looked down in silence, swallowing tears of shame. I glanced at the teacher—a veteran of many years who was rewarded for her teaching abilities by being given the most challenging children each school year. Her classes always had too many students. But she took them all.

Since the children were engaged in their first assignment of the day, I whispered to Mrs. Price, "What are you going to do about her?" I tilted my head toward the pajama-clad child.

She sighed. "Her mom is an addict," she whispered, "and often can't get it together enough to bring her to school. I guess today it was too much trouble to dress her before she dropped her off." Then she added, "I'm going to come up with an excuse to take her to the office. Sometimes we have extra clothes there. If I can't find anything that fits her, I'm going to smile really big and reassure her that the other kids won't notice and tell her how cute her pajamas are."

She stopped then and eye-balled the lady who was part of the administration of this school district and decided to level with me. "You want to know what I'm going to do?" she said. "I'm going to take her the way she came to me and just love her. That's what I do. I take all these children the way they come to me and just love them."

I've thought of that moment so many times since—that feeling you get when you hear an incredible truth. Maybe it's easier to do with kids, but I began to wonder what our lives would be like if we did that with everyone. What if we dropped the pretense and the judgments we make based on the clothes people have on or the cars they drive? What if we really looked into the eyes of those who are trying so hard to impress us and win our favor?

Many people's most obnoxious qualities are really cover-ups for the fear and shame of the little child who still lives inside them. What if we stopped trying to change others and accepted them the way they came to us and just loved them?

> Real love is impossible without forgiveness, and forgiveness is impossible without real love.

So what stands between us and the life we could have? What robs us of peace? I'll tell you in a single word: unforgiveness.

If I had to make a list of the things I really stink at, forgiveness would be at the top of my list. (And, by the way, it would be a very long list.) I know I'm not alone in this as I've heard experts say that in any given demographic group, eighty-five percent of the people are hanging on to a major grudge. I don't have a study with variables and constants and experimental methodology to back this up. But my life experience supports this. Among the people I know (including myself, I confess), airing of grievances consumes a lot of our time. After all, how can you have a satisfying "girls' night out" without dishing the dirt on everyone who's done us wrong?

There is an expression that refusing to forgive is like taking poison and expecting the person you are angry with to die. The toxic effect is on the person who holds the grudge. Often the other person has no idea that you're angry or what you're upset about. Given the dire consequences of harboring grudges, it's amazing that we continue to do it. But we do.

We don't even admit that what we're feeling is anger. Instead we are "hurt." Our self-proclaimed righteous indignation becomes like a cloak we pull tight around us. Instead of warding off the chill in our lives, it adds to it. But abandoning the grievance would feel like a victory for the other team. They don't deserve our forgiveness. If we forgive them, they're off the hook for what they did. And we can't let that happen.

People often say, "I can forgive, but I will never forget." Real forgiveness is like losing your laptop and having no back-up disks. Everything's vanished. Wiped out. Erased from memory with no chance of recovery. Gone in every sense of the word. But who can really do that?

You've probably had awful things happen to you. Maybe far worse than anything I've ever experienced. You were sexually abused. Or the child of an addict. Or someone murdered your son. You might be thinking: *Don't speak to me of forgiveness until you've walked in my shoes.*

Let me tell you about the shoes Jaclyn walks in. She's the only person I've met who seems to have a bigger problem with forgiveness than I do.

When she was in fifth grade, I asked her why she wasn't friends with Amber, a sweet girl in her class.

"When we were at April's birthday party at Chuck E. Cheese, she found the prize tickets I accidentally dropped on the floor and then said they were hers!"

I couldn't even remember April's birthday party. "When was that?"

"When we were in kindergarten."

I laughed. "Five years ago? And you still aren't over it?"

Jaclyn wasn't about to back down. "Well, honestly, what does it say about a person's character if they would do something like that?"

But nothing compared to the anger she harbored toward her birth mother. Jaclyn's mom left her in the woods to die when she was two and a half years old. Jaclyn remembered her last words. She remembered her walking away.

No one knows how long Jaclyn was there, but when a passerby found her, she was so dehydrated she required hospitalization, which is costly and rare in such a poor country. She remembered the IV lines, hooked up to her fragile body, that saved her life.

I don't know all the details of the horror of that experience, but I know the effects. Thirteen years later, she is still terrified of the dark. She can't stand being alone. She can't go upstairs or downstairs in her own home without someone accompanying her. Thirteen years later, she is still afraid.

Many children who are adopted at an older age never speak about their past. Jaclyn was the opposite. She had a long list of grievances, and she demanded to be heard. She had been wronged, and she was quick to finger the guilty. On the top of that list was her birth mother.

In the beginning, I shared her rage. How could a mother have done something so unthinkably cruel? I saw Jaclyn's story through the lens of my Western values and became both judge and jury of Jaclyn's birth mother. And I judged her harshly. I understood she was a poor woman in desperate circumstances. But my heart was outraged. Why didn't she at least take her to the orphanage, where she would be cared for? How could she do something so unspeakably cruel?

Anxious to not lose any of the keys to her past, I journaled daily after I adopted Jaclyn, recording every scrap of memory she shared. Over time, her story came out in bits and pieces.

Jaclyn remembered an infant sister. The girls had different fathers. In China, the law permitted only one child per family. It seemed probable that a mother, forced to choose, would favor the child whose father she was currently in a relationship with. That explained the mother's decision to give up Jaclyn. But it still didn't answer the question of why she didn't take her to an orphanage.

On a return trip to China, I got the key to this mystery. When abandoned children were brought to the orphanage, each child was registered. Part of the registration process was to assign the child a name. The orphanage director told me that Jaclyn's Chinese name, Lou Jiao, was not assigned. It was the name given to her by her birth mother. Jaclyn had revealed it to the policeman who brought her to the orphanage.

In China, it is illegal to abandon a child. Her mother realized that this toddler knew her own name. If she told an orphanage director, who then reported her to the police, the mother could be located and arrested. Then who would care for her new baby? What would happen to her family? Instead of risking that, she did the unthinkable: she took her child to a remote location to die.

When the pieces fit together and I began to understand why, I found myself less filled with judgment. I was, after all, the poster child for white privilege. I'd never for a minute faced the impossible choices Jaclyn's birth mother had. How could I say emphatically what I would do in those circumstances? In extreme poverty? In desperation? In a society with different norms and beliefs?

Who was I to pass judgment, anyway? I thought of the scene in the movie *Sophie's Choice* where the mother is forced by a Nazi officer to choose between her two beloved children. I'll never forget the grief that exploded from her soul in animal-like screams. I no longer judged Jaclyn's birth mother. Instead, I wept for her.

Jaclyn and I had only spoken once of her abandonment. When I tried later to question Jaclyn about it, referring to it as "the time you were lost," she was quick to correct me. "I wasn't lost," she said firmly. "I was waiting for my mama to come back." But we both knew the truth.

When other memories of her birth family surfaced—her anger at not having enough food to eat, her indignation at not having a bed to sleep in—I tried to discuss them logically with her. "China is a very poor country," I said. "Your mom didn't give you more food because she didn't have any." I quickly learned that reason is no match for anger that runs this deep. Forgiveness, if it ever was to be granted, was only hers to bestow. The truth was that I was terrified by the depth of Jaclyn's rage; I backed away.

As the years went by and I became more scarred by my own stubborn refusal to forgive, I began to have small epiphanies about forgiveness. The first one came while I was driving to a doctor's appointment. Driving, by the way, is also on my list of "Things I Really Stink At." I'm not really sure why, and I've run out of excuses. Maybe it's because I don't pay attention as much as I should. Maybe it's a lack of good eye-hand coordination. Maybe it's because those dumb curbs are too close to where I'm driving. In any event, steer clear when you see me coming. Because of my perpetual driving stupidity, I often hear cars honking at me.

One epiphany came after I had made some minor error in judgment merging (that's my story and I'm sticking to it), and I heard protracted honking and glanced in my rearview mirror. The man in the car behind me was in a rage. A full-blown rage. Red faced, arms flailing, hunched over the wheel, shooting daggers at me and looking as if his head would pop off at any minute. And all of a sudden I got it: I didn't intentionally upset him. I didn't even know him. But I made him out-of-control mad because of something stupid I did simply because I wasn't thinking. It was just a "stupid moment." And I was really sorry. But he was so mad at me, he couldn't even begin to comprehend that.

That's how life is sometimes. We do things that make others mad, not intending to be hurtful but because we had a "stupid moment." Words fall out of our mouths that we didn't mean the way they sounded. And we expect to be forgiven.

I began to reflect on the hurtful remarks, the slights, and the comments that had upset me deeply. What if some of them weren't meant to have the effect on me that they did? What if they were the result of others' stupid moments? Why in the world was I hanging on to a grudge over *that*?

Forgiving those we love is much harder than forgiving a stranger or an acquaintance. There seems to be a direct correlation between the depth of our love and the sting of a slight. There is no one whose words can wound deeper than those in our inner circle. Forgiveness here requires us to dig deeper.

But what if I looked at those hurts differently too? Instead of jumping inside the pain and wallowing in it for, oh, about six years, what if I asked myself, "Is it really likely that this person was sitting around the house saying 'Gosh, I wonder what I could say or do to hurt Cindy today?'" What if she was totally clueless about the effect of her words or behavior on me? If insensitivity was the sin, not maliciousness, would it be easier to forgive? What if I took her the way she came to me and just loved her? I was willing to do that with children I barely knew. Why was I unwilling to try it with those I was invested in?

It didn't happen at once, but over time this new perspective became healing. When the "I can't believe she said that" monster reared its ugly head, when the "Why did they do that for her and not for me?" refrain began, I held them back with my new mantra: "No matter what someone says or does, I'm going to take them the way they come to me and love them." And slowly it began to work. Wounds began to scab over when I didn't continuously pick them. Injustices dissolved instead of building up. The thaw began.

Forgiving those I loved was only the beginning. The next step was those who had really wronged me. One man in particular filled me with such hatred, it was as if a black cloud hovered over my soul. The one who had taught me that the taste of fear takes a long time to swallow. I knew I didn't have the power within me to forgive what he'd done. But my soul-searching revealed this truth: if something is beyond my capacity, I need to turn it over to God.

What if I surrendered my rage and simply said, "I don't have the human capacity to forgive *this*. But God, You can do all things. You can even change hearts. Change my heart so I can be released from the power that this unforgiveness has over me." I wondered how it would feel to clear all the anger in my soul.

I sat before the fireplace with my husband one cold, winter morning, and we each wrote down all the hurts we still held on to that we couldn't forgive on our own. We took turns reading aloud each hurt, one at a time, admitting who had inflicted it. Then we released it into the flames, acknowledging that holding on to it was destroying us and keeping us from the life that we wanted. In letting go of the hurts, I freed myself. No one was more surprised than I was when slowly, over time, my heart began to change. Forgiveness had freed me.

That brought me to the final, deepest layer of my unforgiveness pile: forgiving those who had hurt the people I loved. These hurts were much harder to forgive than those inflicted on me personally. I felt powerless against them. And at the top of my list was not Jaclyn's mother, whom I had long ago stopped judging, but the orphanage worker who had beaten Jaclyn.

Jaclyn had told me once, in vivid detail, about being beaten. In a performance that should have garnered me an Academy Award, I had listened to it, keeping my face neutral as I had learned to do so that my distress would not cause her to shut down. I can remember every detail of that recitation like it was yesterday . . . where I was sitting, where she was standing, what the light looked like the moment that my heart froze over.

And then on our second return visit to the orphanage, when Jaclyn reclaimed her beloved charge, the unthinkable happened. Jaclyn looked down into the courtyard and pointed to the culprit. "There she is, Mama," Jaclyn said resolutely. "That's the lady who beat me."

The worker turned, and for a moment, her eyes met mine. Because Jaclyn was speaking English and also because she was so far away, the worker had no idea she'd been outed. And I knew then, in that terrible moment, that we are all capable of murderous rage.

As I struggled on my own road to forgiveness, I had long ago given up on Jaclyn. After the first few years with me, Jaclyn stopped speaking of the woman she called her "China mama." When she was about eight years old, Christy asked her what her China mama was like, and Jaclyn replied, "Now she's just a face." The memories had faded. I dared to hope the rage had as well.

In the fall of Jaclyn's first year of high school, I had an opportunity to hear an author named Mei-Ling Hopgood speak. She has an amazing story. Many years after being privately adopted from Taiwan as an infant, she did the impossible in the world of international adoption: she returned to Taiwan and found her birth family.

That night, as my husband and I excitedly discussed her story, Jaclyn was doing what was pretty much her full-time occupation—hunched over the computer, she was checking Facebook. I didn't think she was listening until she jumped out of her chair as if it were on fire and raced toward me. "Can I do that?" she asked breathlessly. "Would I be able to find my mom?"

In spite of years of justifiable anger, Jaclyn longed to see the woman who'd abandoned her in the woods to die.

Tell me now what it is that you can't forgive.

"And now these three remain: faith, hope and love. But the greatest of these is love" (1 Corinthians 13:13).

Even though the true gifts of life are most visible at the end of our journey, we all hope that our ending is far away and would gladly trade the clarity of perspective for more time. There is only so much time. And nothing drives that home faster than finding out a contemporary is dying. For me, it happened in the fall of

2010 when I heard, through a convoluted grapevine, that my first love, Jim, was rapidly dying of pancreatic cancer.

I met Jim in the fall of my freshman year in college, and because of him I never laugh about "puppy love." You can find your soul mate at eighteen. And know it. Even back then, before life proved me correct, I knew he was extraordinary.

Back in the '70s, with the advent of co-ed dorms in our provincial Midwestern college, we had "visitation hours." At 1:00 a.m. on the dot, the boys had to move to their side of a set of glass double doors and could no longer venture into the girls' portion of the hall- way. But even after spend- ing practically every waking moment together, Jim and I couldn't separate. We'd pull the phone cords into the hall and talk endlessly, struggling

Jim and Cindy as college sweethearts

to glimpse each other through the glass partition that separated us. We celebrated monthly anniversaries with candles stuck in Hostess cupcakes. Our respective roommates gagged constantly, and both refused to room with us the next year. It all sounds crazy and silly now, but back then, I lived for him.

The most vivid memory I have of that time was when I had a big term paper due. I know I'm dating myself by admitting this, but I had an old manual typewriter. Jim's parents had just gifted him with a miraculous new invention: a fancy electric typewriter that had some early word-processor capabilities. He insisted I use it for my project, but I hesitated to borrow something that he had barely used himself. Finally, he convinced me, and I sat down and began banging out my project.

Apparently, I banged too aggressively, because after a few hours the shiny new electric typewriter died. I panicked. I spent several hours trying to figure out how to fix it. When that didn't work, I spent a few more hours thinking about how to break the news to Jim that I had broken his gift.

He came down before dinner and sensed my distress. When I confessed, he looked at me for a long moment. "Is *that* what you're so upset about? The typewriter? Don't you realize I love you? Stuff is stuff. There is no *thing* that means more to me than your feelings." I can still remember that moment. And the one that came after it, when he walked over, pushed the reset button, and fixed the typewriter.

Correction—that isn't my most vivid memory. My most vivid memory is of the day Jim told me he thought we were too serious. We were nineteen. Didn't it just make sense for us to date other people at this stage in our lives? Because it logically made sense did absolutely nothing to mitigate that blow. I can still remember the physical pain of that break-up. I didn't think I'd ever be able to breathe normally again. And when the "other people" Jim decided to date included a gorgeous, blond, upperclassman sorority girl whom I had always suspected he liked, the destruction was complete. I determined never to allow myself to feel that kind of pain again. And I never did.

What I didn't understand then was that this is the double-edged sword of great love—the greater the love, the greater the pain when it falls apart.

Shortly after graduation, Jim moved across the country to California. Twelve years passed as he finished medical school, his internship, and residency. He came back to Michigan to visit once, and we sat together reminiscing in the company of a mutual friend named Sarah. After dinner, he walked me to my car and shared his truth: he had dated a lot. A whole lot. Yep, I figured being a tall, charming, handsome doctor pretty much ensured luck with the ladies. But then he quickly added that although he had dated some special women, he had never loved anyone the way he'd loved me. If I went back to San Diego with him, he promised I'd never want to leave.

I almost laughed out loud. The whole idea was ludicrous. Totally impractical. I was in a serious, committed relationship. I owned my own condo and was established in a really good job. I was so over him. I shook my head and walked away without looking back. Crazy.

A few months later, I told Sarah what had happened. She is a grounded, sensible business executive. I was sure she'd laugh. "You should have gone," she said without hesitation.

A year later, I got up the nerve to mention it to my mom. She was a conservative woman who had taught me to be cautious and careful in my decision making. Without a moment to pause, she said, "You should have gone."

The next time I saw Jim, years later, he had a lovely new bride, Kim, at his side. He had brought her back to Michigan to meet all of his old friends. After dinner, Sarah and I agreed that we liked her even more than we liked him. He'd hit the jackpot. And he deserved it.

Jim, his wife Kim and their children the year before he died

I didn't think it would be fifteen years before I saw him again. I didn't think that was all the time he had left.

When I heard through the college grapevine that Jim was dying, I couldn't believe it. He was a doctor. He was my age. He was living the dream—a beautiful home, married to the love of his life, and father to two children who meant the world to him. All of his dreams had come true. And then, cancer.

I picked up the phone, desperate to find him. After many calls, I finally located a nurse at a hospital who got very quiet when I said his name. I tearfully told this stranger that I was Jim's first love. I heard he had cancer. I needed to talk to him before it was too late. Please, please could she break the rules and tell me how to find him? She whispered a phone number to me and immediately hung up.

With trembling fingers I dialed the number, hoping the news wasn't true. It was.

When I tentatively asked his wife if there was any way I could come out and visit Jim for a few hours, she brushed aside my plan to stay at a hotel and invited me to share her home. "How soon can you get here?" she asked. That's when I knew how bad it really was.

The fear that I wouldn't recognize him after all that time melted the minute I glimpsed the back of a man stooped over his garden. Even from down the street, I recognized him immediately. I had traveled across the country to say "goodbye." He was dying, and we both knew it.

If I felt awkward and a little foolish standing in the doorway of Jim's life with his small children clamoring for attention, my awkwardness faded away under the warm, welcoming embrace of his wife, Kim.

To my surprise, she was wearing a cast on her arm. She waved away my concern. As if caring for one's husband while he's dying wasn't enough of a burden to bear, she had broken her right arm the day before while, ironically, exercising. Her right arm. She is right-handed. And did I mention that she was also caring for an active two-year-old daughter and a high-energy six-year-old son? I'm not sure it gets any worse than that.

I hugged her close and whispered my thanks for the privilege of this visit. No one but Kim would add an ex-girlfriend to this mix. Kim brushed aside my heartfelt words with her gentle humor. "At least all of Jim's old girlfriends are really nice. Honestly, we had four of them at our wedding!" We both burst into giggles, and I was immediately comfortable with this woman I had only met once many years before. Within minutes, I jumped into the thick of things, trying to wrestle a poopy diaper off two-year-old Bianca, who was not at all sure who this stranger was and why her mommy couldn't help her.

Kim and I both knew I was there because she loved Jim and knew what it meant to him to be able to say goodbye to all the people he had loved in his lifetime. I felt lucky to be among those.

A few months before I arrived, a local friend of Jim's had arranged a unique kind of garden party. Jim's friend had rallied all the people who'd asked "What can I do?" when they heard about the devastating illness that had struck this remarkable man. Instead of answering, "Nothing"—the usual response given to those who really want to help—an idea bloomed. What if everyone got together and transformed the hard scrabble backyard they had never gotten around to fixing and made it into a peaceful sanctuary? A place where Jim could sit on a deeply cushioned chaise lounge on a lovely deck, in his last year of living, and enjoy the breeze in the trees and see flowers everywhere and enjoy the incredible California mountain views while watching his children play. A determined army of friends made this vision a reality over one very long weekend.

While publicly expressing gratitude, Jim was privately embarrassed by the hugeness of this gesture. I guess no guy likes to see some other guys spackle his walls. Kim cut that sentiment off at the knees. "This is not about your pride," she told him. "Give your friends the gift of doing for you just as you have done for so many others over the years. Let them do it because they love you and they need a way to show you that love. Live now, in the moment, and when you look around this yard, rejoice in the fact that you are so loved."

Kim was the embodiment of practical wisdom and no-nonsense love. Sometimes it's the hardest thing in the world to receive kindness, and she knew it.

When I stood in the living room and looked through the wall of windows into the backyard, my breath was nearly knocked out of me. I was looking at love manifested, and I had never seen such beauty. I realized in that moment how backward things really are. Why do we bring flowers to the dead instead of to the living? Why do we stand up at funerals and share what our loved ones meant to us after they're gone instead of telling them while they're still alive? That was what brought me to California. I wanted to tell Jim now, while he was still here, what he had meant to me.

The day I arrived happened to be Halloween, so that night we walked through the neighborhood with the little ones to trick-or-treat. All the neighbors were delighted to greet Jim; he obviously had many friends. At one door a woman said, "I can't believe how much Bianca has grown! Last year you had to carry her in your arms. This year she can walk just holding your hand. By next year . . . " She stopped short. We were all thinking the same thing. *Next year you won't be here with her.*

Over the weekend, partially because Kim is a saint and partially because she was sleepy from the pain medication for her broken arm, Jim and I spent hours talking while we watched the kids play. In spite of what he was dealing with, Jim wanted to hear about my challenges, what had happened in my life, how I was doing. Somehow he found the stamina in his depleted supply of energy to listen for the pain behind the words. Basking in his sensitivity, I forgot for a few moments that this visit wasn't about me.

Eventually the talk shifted to his life and his dying. He talked in the easy way you can with a person who once knew you so well and who now was really a stranger. He told me he had no regrets—he did work that he loved, he found purpose in serving others, he waited to marry until he found the woman of his dreams. He said he hadn't been sure how he would know whether someone was the right girl for him—the person who had everything on his list. But when he met Kim, he realized there was no list. She had qualities he hadn't even known to look for. His beautiful son and daughter were the icing on the cake. He had everything he had ever dreamed of and more.

No regrets? I could hardly fathom it. My own pile of regrets was so high I wouldn't even know where to begin to catalog them.

I asked him if he was at peace. I wondered if he was angry with God. After all, it seemed especially cruel to be one of the few who had it all and then have it so abruptly grabbed away.

He smiled. "I see it the exact opposite way. The question isn't why this terrible illness happened to me. The real question I wrestle with is how I got so lucky as to have the life I've had."

We spoke of heaven as a place of perfect peace. As someone who liked a scientific explanation for all things, Jim was struggling to sort out what he believed. Then he confessed that he hadn't been entirely honest, he did have one regret: he wished he'd had his children when he was younger. That was the one thing standing between him and peace. It wasn't a question of what would become of his kids—they had a wonderful mom. But didn't we make a promise to kids when we gave them life that we would be there for them? *What would be left of him when he was gone? What would remain?* His two-year-old daughter probably wouldn't even remember him.

I listened silently and thought, yes, we do promise our children a certain life when we welcome them into the world. In fact, we make all kinds of promises. That we will be there when they take their first steps. That we will be there when they fall. That we'll be there. But the One who gives life makes no such promises. We can't see the end; we can only see the now.

Overwhelmed by emotion, I needed to leave. The knowledge that this was "goodbye" was suffocating. I'd had no idea how hard it would be to watch someone I'd loved dying. I moved up my flight. For a guilty moment, I realized how lucky I was that I hadn't gone with him to San Diego all

Jim and Cindy at their final visit

those years ago . . . because then I would be in Kim's place, and there was no way I could be her.

When I hugged him goodbye, I whispered in his ear, "I'll see you on the other side." I take comfort in that promise of my faith. I hoped he believed it too.

When I got home, weary with jet lag and flight delays, I found a bag of Halloween candy on my bed. Puzzled, I told Christy she'd left some of her candy in my room. "Oh, no, Mom, that's for *you*," she explained. "I traded my Halloween candy to get as many Twizzlers and bubble gums as I could because I know those are your favorites." I think that was the most loving gesture I have ever been the recipient of.

And then I knew the answer to Jim's question about what remains behind after we die. This is what is left of us when we leave this earth: our love.

The Ultimate Gift

Peace is the last gift on my list because, except for the very wise, most people don't find it until later in life. But it is the ultimate gift.

In the end, the only way to die in peace is to have lived in peace. To be grateful for all the events of our past—both good and bad—that brought us to the place we are on that final day. To cherish perfect moments. To be happy right where we are. To see the best and forget the rest. To love with open arms. To never miss a chance to hug our kids. To believe that all things are possible. To have tried to make a difference. To speak the truth. To trust that God will make everything right and keep us safe. To know that it mattered that we lived because we are part of a bigger plan. To be slow to anger and gentle with others. To be gentle with ourselves. To strive to be our best selves but to forgive ourselves when we fall short. To forgive those who don't deserve it.

To embrace these truths is to embrace the gift of peace.

Peace be with you.

Acknowledgements

When you work for God, I guess that is really the only acknowledgement that you need. I didn't write a word of this book; the Holy Spirit led me, and I have to admit that I wasn't always the most cooperative participant in this project. In fact, the guidance was so complete that afterward I often read sections that didn't even seem familiar to me. I thank God for the privilege of being his servant and for using my humble gifts to touch others.

That being said, the inspiration for doing this book came solely from my kids in Kenya. Through a wonderful organization called Warm Blankets Orphan Care, these kids dove into my heart to such a degree that when I close my eyes, I see their faces. This book is dedicated to raising both funds and awareness for those who have no voice. If you want to partner with my family in this cause, check out our orphan home: http://ourlegacy.orphanmissions.com/index.htm. It is my honor and privilege to use my gifts to serve them; I can think of no higher purpose.

If my faith has taught me anything, it is that God doesn't work alone. So I need to acknowledge the lady who coached me through the angst of book-writing: Kathy Anderson. The unlikely way that we met so many years ago and the fact that you popped up in my inbox at just the time I needed someone to encourage me through the muck is further evidence that there is a plan. God gave you the words I needed to hear more times than

I can count. Thank you, Kathy. And if anyone needs a talented life coach, contact Kathy @:ka_ftc@mac.com

I also want to acknowledge my editor, Brenda Covert, and Tim Lowry of Ambassador International and thank them for their efforts in bringing my story to you.

It is a fallacy that this book is a compilation of the stories of my life. Thankfully, none of us walk alone. This book is really a compilation of the intersection of many lives with my own. I am honored to call as friends the individuals whose stories are also told in this book:

Danna Autrey, the one who held my hand in some of my darkest hours. Snow Wu, the courageous lady who brought Christy, Jaclyn, and so many other special children into my life. Marcee Martin, the greatest boss I ever had and the kindest spirit I have ever known. Mrs. Vogel, Miss Kerri, and Lisa Adams—you'll never know the impact you had on my kids and on me too. Dee Hinger who personifies "it takes a village." Teresa Schwartz, the eternal optimist. Melanie Parks for encouraging me at the start of my adoption journey. Julie, Mark, and Lynn Mei—I'll never forget you. Heidi Hales—the greatest child advocate I have ever known. God smiles when he looks down upon you, girlfriend. Kim Manning—an unlikely friend by any definition of the word. I hope we did Jim proud. Deb Morse and the entire Mero family. Thanks for adopting me into your family. Thinking of your dad always makes me smile. Ed and Sue and the entire Griffen family—I understand why my kids got so mad when I tried to suggest that we aren't really related. Not a drop of common blood between us, but if family are the people who stand shoulder to shoulder with you, you are my family. When I look at all the pictures of family fun over the years, Griffens are in nearly all of them. I can't even imagine a life without Camp Griffen. I love you all.

The "Albion girls" have always supported and encouraged me and listened to my endless stories, and for that there aren't enough words of thanks. Deb, Diana, and Sarah—you really know me and, amazingly, still love me. And you never say I'm crazy. At least to my face.

And what would my life be without the support of the "Internet girls." Pam, Kate, Sally, Liz, and Kathy—you walk every day with me. You experience my ups and down. You encourage me. You give me advice. You listen. I wouldn't make it without you.

A special thanks to my parents—Don and Ruth Schmidt. Seeing your excitement every step of the way makes it all so much fun. You always think I am capable of so much more than I really am. Thanks for believing in me.

As for my darling Joe, there aren't sufficient words to really thank you. Thank you for loving me. Thank you for loving our daughters as your own. Thank you for always telling me that you feel like the luckiest man on earth. I know we don't have enough years left together on this earth, but I can't wait to spend eternity with you. Gate #8. Be there or be square.

My beautiful Kate. I want to be just like you when I grow up. There is no one on this earth who could have gone from a doted-upon only child to a big sister to two new siblings within one and a half years with such a loving and selfless heart. Every kid should have a sister like you. Every mom should have a daughter like you.

My precious Christy. The luckiest day I ever had was the day I became your mom. You are everything to me. You always will be.

And finally, first, last and always, my thanks are for Jaclyn. Life has knocked you but never knocked you down. For your courage in sharing your story with others, you will always be my hero. And to think that I once believed we teach our children.

ALL of the proceeds from this book are designated for the Warm Blankets Orphan Care home in Kenya:
http://ourlegacy.orphanmissions.com/index.htm

Book Club Questions

1. What is your favorite anecdote in the book? Why?

2. In the preface, the author asks the question: "What you would tell your twenty-year-old self if you could go back in time?" How would you answer that?

3. In sharing the brutal reality of Jaclyn's past, the author asserts that these horrific events brought with them gifts too (i.e., "Even a heart that's been broken can love hugely"). Do you agree that tough times are often bundled with powerful lessons? Have you ever experienced a difficulty in your own life that later proved to be an important life lesson?

4. The author writes: "We are not meant to live as timid mice, frantically trying to find our way around a maze filled with road blocks. We are meant to live as explorers on an adventure, trusting in the One who holds the map." Have you seen evidence in your own life that there is a greater plan?

5. The chapter on "Perfect Moments" suggests that it is really a myth that one can have a happy life but that happy moments are more realistic. Do you agree? Is it unrealistic to strive for a happy life?

6. The author shares some of her own lessons learned as a parent (i.e., "I've learned that sometimes, what is unsaid matters most" and "I've learned that you can have success in mothering just by showing up and trying your best"). What has been the best lesson you have learned from parenting?

7. In the chapter "Pathways and Possibilities," the author relates the unexpected altering in her life path that followed Jaclyn's adoption. Has your life followed the path you expected? If not, what changed it?

8. The author states that our greatest purpose is often found in our smallest acts of kindness. Is this how you see your life's purpose? How would you define it?

9. Using Jaclyn's example of refusing to rationalize George Washington's decision to be a slave owner, the author asserts that sharing your own truth is liberating. Have you ever been faced with a situation that conflicted with your own truth? How have you handled that?

10. In the chapter "Partners and Protectors," the author suggests that the people who are there for you in difficult times may not be your family members. How does this match your life experience? Who has been your support network in challenging circumstances?

11. The author gives several accounts of the power of prayer, including the miraculous healing of her youngest daughter. Have you ever experienced anything you would consider to be miraculous? How has prayer impacted you?

For more information about
CINDY CHAMPNELLA
&
THE TWELVE GIFTS OF LIFE:
FINDING EXTRAORDINARY MEANING
IN ORDINARY MOMENTS
please visit:

www.cindychampnella.com
cindycindy3333@yahoo.com

For more information about
AMBASSADOR INTERNATIONAL
please visit:

www.ambassador-international.com
@AmbassadorIntl
www.facebook.com/AmbassadorIntl